DK GARDEN GUIDES

CONSERVATORY
& HOUS S

KT-434-920

Moreton Morrell Site

RICHARD ROSENFELD

DK

A DORLING KINDERSLEY BOOK
Moreton Morrell Site

DK

**LONDON, NEW YORK,
MUNICH, MELBOURNE, DELHI**

Series Editor Helen Fewster
Series Art Editor Alison Donovan
Project Editor Zia Allaway
Designer Rachael Smith
Editor Robin Pridy
Managing Editor Anna Kruger
Managing Art Editor Lee Griffiths
Consultant Louise Abbott
DTP Designer Louise Waller
Media Resources Lucy Claxton
Picture Research Carolyn Clerkin
Production Controller Mandy Inness

First published in Great Britain in 2004 by
Dorling Kindersley Limited
80 Strand, London, WC2R ORL
A Penguin company

A CIP catalogue record for this book is available
from The British Library
ISBN 0 7513 3878 8

Colour reproduction by Colourscan, Singapore
Printed and bound by Printer Trento, Italy

see our complete catalogue at
www.dk.com

Growing conservatory and houseplants

Living rooms and conservatories are a great way of bringing the garden indoors. They also provide a terrific opportunity to grow tender plants that won't survive outside, and by using a lively mix of the well-known and rare, you can easily create a dash of the tropics. If you want fresh lemons, snapping Venus fly traps, delicate orchids, cactuses with bright punchy flowers, powerfully-scented gardenias, and South American jaborosas, read on.

Feature plants

Gardening indoors is much like gardening outside – with a large space, you can create schemes with big star plants, climbers, lots of rich colour, small fillers for the front, and fun plants to perk things up. One of the most striking, "must-have", large conservatory plants is to use as a focal point is the exotic crane flower (*Strelitzia reginae*), which resembles a fabulous bird's head and is surprisingly easy to grow. Other star plants include the chunky Brazilian shrub, yesterday, today and tomorrow (*Brunfelsia pauciflora*), whose mass of flowers turns from purple to mauve and white, and the elephant foot tree (*Nolinia recurvata*), with its long, bare stem and wild array of thin leaves.

When you've chosen key plants for a specific theme, the next step is to decide what to group around them.

◀ **The crane flower** (*Strelitzia reginae*) is a stunning conservatory plant with bright flowerheads that resemble an exotic bird's head.

▶ **The elephant foot tree** (*Nolinia recurvata*), is a real show-stopper.

Even the humble mind-your-own-business (*Soleirolia soleirolii*) looks stylish in smart white pots set a row.

Rich and sweet

Jasmine and daturas add instant exotica, with *Jasminum polyanthum* twining and twisting up wall wires or spiralling around a pillar. Daturas (*Brugmansia*) are amongst the many pot plants that enjoy being stood outdoors over summer. *Brugmansia* X *candida* 'Grand Marnier', also known as angels' trumpet, is a stunner, with splendidly large, felt-like leaves, and apricot flowers that emit a gorgeous rich scent in the evening.

Other choices for good scent include

◀ **Freesia 'Blue Heaven'** is just one of the range of sweetly-scented freesias.

freesias (in a wide colour range), *Heliotropium arborescens*, and the wax plant (*Hoya carnosa*) which has stiff-petalled, white flowers with a smart red eye. The blooms of Kahili ginger (*Hedychium gardnerianum*) appear in late summer and have a fantastic scent, too.

Flowers and colour

As well as scented plants, you also need stunning flowers and colours. The orchids include some absolute beauties, such as *Pleione formosana*, many of which do not need a high-tech, humid conservatory, and can be grown easily on a windowsill. Also look out for the calico flower (*Aristolochia littoralis*) with its bizarre yellow, purple and brown mottled flowers; peering into the flared open end of a bloom is like looking into a curved smoker's pipe. For rich blues, go for the Brazilian spider flower (*Tibouchiana urvilleana*) with its royal purple flowers; for magenta-red, try *Bougainvillea* 'Scarlett O'Hara'; and for flashy yellow, there is the magnificent golden trumpet (*Allamanda cathartica*).

Add impact with the royal blue flowers of *Tibouchiana*.

Startling leaves

Many plants are worth growing simply for their impressive leaves, and there is a long list to choose from. Just flick through the first few pages of this book and you will find a good selection, including the alocasias, many with giant arrow-shaped leaves; caladiums, such as angel wings (*Caladium bicolor*) with its rich pink and red foliage; the Japanese fatsia (*Fatsia japonica*), a vastly under-rated plant with impressive, glossy leaves; and a wide variety of bromeliads, found in the wild growing deep in rainforests, with their striped, flashy leaves.

Angel wings (*Caladium bicolor*) has heart-shaped, exquisitely-coloured leaves.

For adults, there are citrus trees – actually bushy shrubs for pots or conservatory borders – which produce a big supply of fresh lemons and kumquats. In fact, there is a whole range of plants that will bear fruit, from hot peppers to bunches of grapes. On a more modest note, the spider plant (*Chlorophytum comosum* 'Vittatum') is an extraordinary sight in a hanging pot in midsummer with its 'umbilical' cords shooting out over the sides, baby plants dangling in the air. Easy to find, easy to grow and, like many in this book, a great way of livening up your indoor space.

Fun plants

Good ideas for children include carnivorous plants, from the surprisingly easy-to-grow Venus fly trap (*Dionaea muscipula*), which snaps shut on beetles and spiders (and doesn't need a hothouse atmosphere), to the *Nepenthes* x *hookerinana*, which entices insects to fall inside its elongated, nectar-filled pouches, where they are dissolved into a kind of nutritious 'soup'. Other fun plants for small people include the artillery plant (*Pilea microphylla*), which just needs a quick shake in summer to make the pollen fly up like canon smoke.

Growing fruit indoors will add a dash of colour, and edible lemons, kumquats, olives or grapes.

Where to grow houseplants

Conservatories are ideal environments for houseplants because you can gear the conditions exactly to the plants' needs – in the home, plants must fit in with your requirements. But homes do offer different conditions: bathrooms have good humidity (ideal for ferns); windowsills provide bright light (good for herbs); and bedrooms give the stable temperatures that many plants enjoy. If a plant is not happy in one room, move it to another with different conditions.

Culinary herbs are perfect for kitchen windows.

Bathrooms are perfect places for plants that enjoy a warm, humid atmosphere, such as ferns and yuccas.

Conservatories offer ideal conditions for a wide range of exotics. Create a year-round display of foliage plants mixed with colourful, scented flowers, and try to ensure that they all enjoy similar conditions.

Houseplant hates Houseplants generally cannot tolerate the relentless, hot, dry conditions of a centrally-heated home, temperature fluctuations, cold draughts, and being scorched by the hot summer sun through a window. Poor light can also result in stressed, feeble growth.

The growing guide – key tips

Most plants need bright light to manufacture food and release energy (those with coloured or variegated leaves need high light levels). A few, such as cactuses and succulents, cope with direct sun, but the rest prefer indirect light away from a window, but not in shade. Plants grow towards the light, so turn them every few days for even growth. Note, too, that the heights and spreads given in this book are dimensions for pot-grown plants.

Ventilation and humidity

Most plants like decent ventilation in summer – standing them outside helps, but wait until the weather is warm enough. Some will need high humidity, especially when temperatures rise. To create this, stand the pot on pebbles (*see below*) or mist your plants with a spray (use rainwater or cold boiled water to avoid chemical deposits from tap water on the leaves). Grouping plants together also helps to create a humid environment.

Increase humidity by standing plants on a tray filled with pebbles and water.

Watering

The general rule is to water plants regularly when they are in full growth, but water less frequently when they are dormant – when the temperature falls and growth stops, plants are not so thirsty. To avoid overwatering – one of the most frequent causes of pot plant death – play it safe and wait until the compost

Avoid spillages by filliing the saucer with water, rather than watering the soil.

is nearly dry before giving the next drink. When watering, wait until the water runs out of the drainage holes before applying more. Acid-loving plants need soft water.

Cleaning leaves

Some indoor plants will become very dusty in a surprisingly short space of time – this is particularly noticeable on plants with large, glossy foliage. To clean them, wipe with a soft, damp cloth, or stand them outside on warm, rainy days in summer.

To remove dust wipe the leaves with a soft, damp cloth, but try to avoid the new young foliage.

The right pot

As plants grow, they will need to be moved every few years in the spring into larger pots (potting on). To check if this is necessary, remove the plants from their pots to see if the roots are congested and starting to poke out of the drainage holes. The new, clean container should be one or two sizes larger than the old. Moving plants into excessively large pots is counter-

productive because the roots may end up sitting in cold, damp soil for long periods, especially over winter, which leads to rot.

If plants grow too quickly, take up too much space and need to be moved regularly into larger pots, keep them in the same size pot to restrain growth – also restrict them by pruning the root system each spring.

Terracotta pots are heavy and less likely to get knocked over. They also absorb moisture which means that plants grown in terracotta pots need to be watered more often than those in plastic pots, which are not porous.

◀ **Mediterranean palms**, which can be fast growing, may be restrained by keeping them in a small pot.

How to pot on

1 Check pot size
Select a pot that is one or two sizes larger than the original. Clean the new pot with disinfectant.

2 Soak root ball
Put the plant in a bucket of water. The roots will draw up water through the drainage hole.

3 Loosen roots
Remove the plant from the pot and gently tease out roots that are packed tightly around the edges.

4 Repot
Place plant in the new pot. Infill with the same type of compost as before, and plant at the same depth.

Potting up and choosing compost

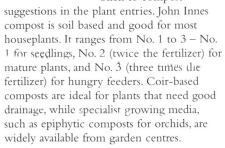

Houseplant compost

Coir bulb fibre

All plant containers must have holes at the bottom, which should be covered with crocks or polystyrene chips to prevent the soil washing out and to aid drainage. Soak the plant for an hour before potting it up (*see below left*). Put a layer of compost over the crocks, insert the plant, and ensure that the top of the soil is 5cm (2in) below the pot's rim to allow for watering. Stick to compost suggestions in the plant entries. John Innes compost is soil based and good for most houseplants. It ranges from No. 1 to 3 – No. 1 for seedlings, No. 2 (twice the fertilizer) for mature plants, and No. 3 (three times the fertilizer) for hungry feeders. Coir-based composts are ideal for plants that need good drainage, while specialist growing media, such as epiphytic composts for orchids, are widely available from garden centres.

Feeding

Foliar feeds give flagging plants an instant lift.

Nutrients in compost wash out after a while, and plants then need to be fed during their growing season. Add an all-purpose liquid feed to the water or use a slow-release fertilizer. For extra flowers and fruit, use a tomato feed; nitrogen fertilizers are best for foliage plants. Do not feed in autumn or winter when plants are dormant.

Training

Small climbers are trained easily over a wire hoop.

In a conservatory, large, vigorous climbers can be trained up horizontal wires fixed to the wall, while smaller climbers may be grown up canes or wire loops. Train plants with aerial roots up moss poles – spray them regularly with water to increase humidity.

Pruning

Snip off shoot tips to increase bushiness

Pruning helps to create an evenly-shaped plant, stimulates bushy growth, and restricts the size of large climbers

and shrubs. Prune in spring, cutting back the stems to a bud that points outwards. Older, straggly plants will benefit from a hard prune to encourage new, bushy growth. You can also promote denser growth on young plants, and prevent them from getting straggly, by snipping off the tips of young stems.

What went wrong?

If plants are grown well, watered regularly, and given the correct amount of food and light, they should flourish, but setbacks can still occur. Most problems can be remedied easily by changing the position of the plant or watering frequency.

Lack of water

When a plant collapses and drops its flowers and leaves, it may be suffering from a lack of water. The simple solution is to water it, but if the soil has dried out completely, it may shrink away from the side of the pot, leaving a gap. To prevent water from sluicing straight through the gap when you give the plant a drink, plunge it into a bucket of water and submerge it up to the stem. Hold down the pot until there are no more air bubbles. If there's still a gap at the side of the pot, push the compost out with your fingers, or fill in the gap with fresh soil.

Wilting is often due to a lack of water.

Overwatering

Wilting stems and yellowing leaves, poor growth and moss growing on the compost are often signs of overwatering. To help remedy this situation, remove the plant from its pot and allow the moisture in the soil to evaporate. When it feels slightly moist but not wet, put it back in its pot.

To prevent this from happening again, allow the top layer of soil to dry out before applying another drink, and ensure that the pot is not sitting in a saucer of water. Also check that the pot is not too large for the plant, which can result in moisture being retained in the excess compost. If this is the case, remove the plant from the container, gently tap off some of the soil from around the rootball and replace it in a smaller pot.

Over- and underfeeding

Weak, thin, spindly growth, aphid and whitefly infestations and yellowing leaves may indicate overfeeding. Do not feed for a few weeks to give the plant a chance to rest, but water as usual to flush out any chemicals; then adopt the appropriate regime.

Plants that have not been fed while in full growth may grow poorly or develop yellow areas between the leaf veins. This is known as chlorosis and indicates a lack of iron or magnesium. Rectify this by applying houseplant fertilizer (or sequestrene for acid lovers).

Scorched leaf caused by overfeeding

Pest and diseases

It is a good idea to check your plants every few days for signs of pests and diseases, and deal with any problems promptly. Healthy plants are less vulnerable to attack, but if yours do succumb, most pests and diseases can be treated with chemical sprays; ensure you read the manufacturer's instructions carefully before use. Aphids can be picked off, or take the affected plant outside and spray with a hose to remove them.

Whitefly
Colonies of tiny white insects that suck the sap of leaves and stems. Use biological controls or spray with pyrethrum.

Aphids
Tiny sap-sucking insects that cluster on stems and the undersides of leaves. Pick off by hand or spray with pyrethrum.

Red spider mites
Create mottling on upper surface of leaves; mites like hot, dry conditions. Increase humidity, and spray with bifenthrin.

Scale insects
Appear on undersides of foliage, stems, and veins, and leave a sticky deposit on the leaves. Spray plant with malathion.

Mealybugs
Sap-sucking insects that are covered with a white fluffy substance. Use biological controls or spray with malathion.

Downy Mildew
Yellow spots on leaf surfaces and grey mould underneath. Remove affected parts and spray with a fungicide.

Powdery mildew
Covers the leaves initially, then other areas, with a greyish-white powder. Remove affected parts and spray with fungicide.

Sooty Mould
Black fungus that grows on the secretions left by sap-sucking insects. Wipe off with a damp cloth, or remove affected parts.

A–Z of Conservatory & Houseplants

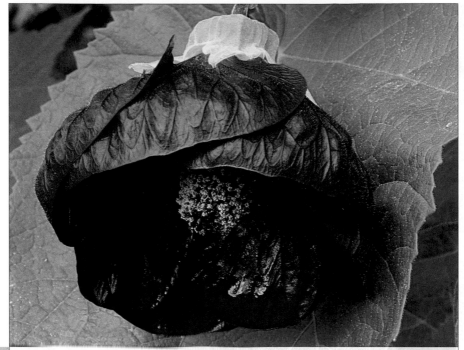

A | *Abutilon* 'Nabob' Flowering maple

THE EYE-CATCHING, DARK RED BELL-LIKE FLOWERS of 'Nabob' dangle from the thin, woody horizontal branches attached to its vertical main stem. The evergreen leaves resemble the foliage on a maple, hence the common name. This easily-grown abutilon is invaluable in a large conservatory (trained against a wall or supported by a stout cane), adding height and attractive leafy growth, and flowers that appear over a long summer season. Water freely when in full growth and apply a monthly liquid feed; water sparingly over winter when dormant. Prune lightly in early spring to improve its shape and remove straggly growth. Beware whitefly.

OTHER VARIETIES *A.* 'Canary Bird' (red flowers); *A. megapotamicum* (red and yellow flowers).

PLANT PROFILE
HEIGHT 1.8m (6ft)
SPREAD 1.8m (6ft)
SITE Full light
SOIL John Innes No. 2
HARDINESS Half hardy
FLOWERING Spring to autumn

Acacia pravissima Ovens wattle

A

IN THE WILD, THIS AUSTRALIAN SHRUB or small tree is quite large, reaching 8m (25ft) high, but it will also thrive indoors in a large pot. The arching graceful growth has evergreen triangular leaves (strictly speaking, they are leaf stalks) and clusters of sweetly-scented bright yellow flowers that look like pompoms. This plant requires plenty of space and is often trained against a wall. Give a light (definitely not hard) prune after flowering for shape and space, if required. Water well in the growing season and provide a monthly liquid feed, but water sparingly in winter. Red spider mites may be a problem.

OTHER VARIETIES *A. baileyana* 'Purpurea' (fern-like purple-tinted leaves); *A. dealbata* (silvery leaves, scented flowers).

PLANT PROFILE	
HEIGHT 5m (18ft)	
SPREAD 1.8m (6ft)	
SITE Full light	
SOIL John Innes No. 2	
HARDINESS Half hardy	
FLOWERING Late winter and spring	

A   *Acalypha wilkesiana* 'Can-can' Copperleaf

GROWN FOR ITS ATTRACTIVE, DARK COPPERY FOLIAGE, 'Can-can' is
related to the spreading shrub, *A. wilkesiana*, which grows wild in
the Pacific Islands and has multi-coloured, often variegated leaves
and long catkin-like flowers. 'Can-can' is slightly different because it
is not grown for its catkins but for its coloured leaves, which are
serrated, slightly red at the margin and about 15cm (6in) long. If it
becomes straggly, prune in spring. Keep 'Can-can' in bright light for
the best leaf colour, and water freely in the growing season. Apply a
monthly liquid feed in summer and water moderately in winter. In
spring, move to a larger pot or replace the top layer of soil.

OTHER VARIETIES   *A. hispida* (rich green leaves and fluffy red
catkins); *A. wilkesiana* (multi-coloured leaves, with catkins).

PLANT PROFILE

HEIGHT To 1.8m (6ft)

SPREAD To 1–2m (3–6ft)

SITE Full light

SOIL Loamless potting
compost

HARDINESS Min 10°C
(50°F)

FLOWERING Periodically

Achimenes hybrids Hot water plant

A

PLANTS WITH A LONG FLOWERING SEASON are a big bonus, and the dozens of hybrid achimenes have the advantage of being easily grown. The flowers come in yellow, pink, purple, blue and white, and though the individual blooms do not last long (just a few days), a profusion of buds prolongs the flowering period, giving great value for money. Water from spring on, freely over summer, applying a quarter-strength liquid feed each time. Remove the dead top growth in the autumn, and store dry in a container at 10°C (50°F) until spring. It will start into growth again when the temperature reaches 16–18°C (61–64°F). Prone to aphids and red spider mites.

OTHER VARIETIES *A.* 'Little Beauty' (dark green leaves, deep pink flowers); *A.* 'Peach Blossom' (magenta-pink flowers).

PLANT PROFILE
HEIGHT 30cm (12in)
SPREAD 30cm (12in)
SITE Bright filtered light
SOIL John Innes No.2
HARDINESS Min 10–15°C (50–59°F)
FLOWERING Summer to autumn

A

Adiantum raddianum Delta maidenhair fern

ELEGANT, LIGHT AND AIRY, this tropical American evergreen fern has a lovely mound of gently arching, black wiry stems that are covered with tiny delicate leaves (fronds). But note that it does need special conditions. The soil needs extra peat and even sharp sand to guarantee good drainage, while the atmosphere should be quite humid with good ventilation. Provide indirect bright light, but do not let the plants bake in direct sun; also avoid draughts. Water well in full growth, giving a monthly, half-strength liquid feed. It is a good choice for planting in a terrarium (a large, enclosed glass or plastic container or bottle).

OTHER VARIETIES *A. raddianum* 'Elegans' (shorter fronds); *A. raddianum* 'Fritz Lüthi' (light green fronds).

PLANT PROFILE

HEIGHT To 60cm (24in)

SPREAD 80cm (32in)

SITE Bright light

SOIL 1 part compost and peat substitute to 2 parts sharp sand and 3 parts leafmould

HARDINESS Min 7°C (45°F)

Aechmea recurvata

THIS EVERGREEN BROMELIAD grows in the wild in South American rainforests, where the moisture drips down into its central cup of leaves. The plant has a rosette of tough, dark or mid-green leaves about 40cm (16in) long that are fringed by tiny spines. The pinkish-white or purple flowers, which last for several weeks, are followed by small, round, white fruit. Water freely in the growing season and apply a diluted nitrogen fertilizer each month. Keep the central cup filled with rain- or soft water. Beware scale insects and mealybugs.

OTHER VARIETIES *A. fasciata* (blue flowers, other parts pink); *A. morganii* (glossy leaves, blue flowers, other parts pink).

PLANT PROFILE
HEIGHT To 20cm (8in)
SPREAD To 50cm (20in)
SITE Bright filtered light
SOIL Epiphytic compost
HARDINESS Min 10°C (50°F)
FLOWERING Summer

A

Aeonium 'Zwartkop'

A STRIKING ARCHITECTURAL SUCCULENT, *A.* 'Zwartkop' is easy to grow in a pot. The pencil-thin bare stems, which become nicely branched with just a few off-shoot stems, are topped by rosettes of near-black fleshy leaves up to 15cm (6in) long, but the plant needs to be at least four years old before the yellow flowers appear. 'Zwartkop' may become top-heavy and fall over, especially if kept outside in summer. To avoid this, use a chunky clay pot instead of a lightweight plastic one. Water freely when in full growth, but let the soil dry out between waterings; give a liquid feed two to three times in summer and keep dry in winter. Beware greenfly and mealybugs.

OTHER VARIETIES *A. arboreum* (spoon-shaped light green leaves); *A. arboreum* 'Atropurpureum' (purple-red leaves).

PLANT PROFILE
HEIGHT 90cm (3ft)
SPREAD 90cm (3ft)
SITE Bright filtered light
SOIL Standard cactus compost
HARDINESS Min 10°C (50°F)
FLOWERING Late spring

Aeschynanthus Black Pagoda Group

A

THE SEMI-TRAILING GROWTH of Black Pagoda Group, which is covered by pale green, 10cm (4in) long leaves with dark brown marbling, makes it a good choice for a hanging basket. The attractive, 5cm (2in) long, thin burnt-orange flowers appear at the ends of the stems in groups of three or four, but the plant needs to be grown in a humid conservatory to provide a good display. Give it a regular supply of rainwater or soft water when in full growth and apply a monthly, weak liquid feed to established plants; water sparingly over winter. If the plant starts getting straggly, cut it back slightly in the spring or autumn. Aphids may be a problem.

OTHER VARIETIES *A. longicaulis* (orange-red flowers); *A. pulcher* (red flowers); *A. speciosus* (bright orange flowers).

PLANT PROFILE

HEIGHT 60cm (24in)

SPREAD To 45cm (18in)

SITE Bright filtered light

SOIL 3 parts peat substitute to 1 part sphagnum moss

HARDINESS Min 15–18°C (59–64°F)

FLOWERING Summer

A

Aglaonema 'Silver Queen'

A STRONGLY-COLOURED, SLOW-GROWING PLANT for the style conscious, 'Silver Queen' has bright green variegated leaves that grow to about 30cm (12in) long (*see inset*). They are the big attraction; the infrequent flowers do not amount to much. Because the parent plants come from tropical Asian forests, where they grow in low light levels, 'Silver Queen' must be kept out of bright light. It also needs free-draining soil, which is best achieved by mixing horticultural grit to the compost to open it up. Provide humidity and water moderately (more sparingly over winter). Apply a monthly liquid feed in spring and summer.

OTHER VARIETY *A.* 'Malay Beauty' (white stems with green marbling and green mottled leaves).

PLANT PROFILE

HEIGHT 60cm (24in)

SPREAD 45cm (18in)

SITE Filtered light

SOIL John Innes No. 2 or 3

HARDINESS Min 13°C (55°F)

FLOWERING Summer or autumn

Allamanda cathartica Golden trumpet

A MAGNIFICENTLY VIGOROUS CLIMBER, the golden trumpet is native to the swamps of Central and South America, where it can reach 15m (50ft) and is covered by trumpet-like, scented, flashy yellow flowers. Confined in a conservatory pot, the growth is much more modest, and it is best trained against a wall with a system of horizontal wires leading up to the roof. The best time to thin out or cut back, if required, is in late summer. Provide summer humidity (less so in winter when the temperature drops). Water freely in full growth, giving a liquid feed every two to three weeks; water sparingly in winter. Prone to red spider mites and whiteflies.

OTHER VARIETY *A. cathartica* 'Grandiflora' (glossy leaves; needs min. temperature of 15°C/59°F).

PLANT PROFILE

HEIGHT 4.5m (13½ft)

SPREAD 2m (6ft)

SITE Bright light

SOIL John Innes No. 3

HARDINESS Min 7–10°C (45–50°F)

FLOWERING Summer to autumn

A

Alocasia cuprea Elephant's ear plant

THE ALOCASIAS ARE SPECTACULAR FOLIAGE PLANTS, many with giant arrow-shaped leaves and vivid patterning. The elephant's ear plant has superb, dark green leaves, which, in the wild, can reach 1.2m (4ft) long, with raised areas between the veins (*see inset*). Allow plenty of room for the foliage to spread out in the conservatory, where high humidity is essential in full growth. Water freely and apply a liquid fertilizer every two to three weeks over summer; water moderately in winter. This alocasia is not widely sold, but can be tracked down easily. Protect against mealybugs. All parts are toxic.

OTHER VARIETY *A. x amazonica* (extraordinary, eye-catching bright white veins set in dark green leaves).

PLANT PROFILE
HEIGHT 1m (3ft)
SPREAD 75cm (30in)
SITE Filtered light
SOIL Equal parts composted bark, loam and sand
HARDINESS Min 15–18°C (59–64°F)

Alocasia macrorrhiza Giant taro

A

AN EXOTIC PLANT grown for its highly impressive, glossy leaf blades which, in the wild, may reach 1.2m (4ft) long. Make sure there is plenty of room in the conservatory for the leaves to spread out and be seen clearly, and maintain high humidity through the growing season. Water freely and apply a liquid fertilizer every two to three weeks over summer, but water moderately in winter. Giant taro is not sold by many nurseries, but it is available. Avoid contact with the sap as this can irritate the skin; all parts will upset the stomach if eaten. Giant taro is susceptible to mealybugs.

OTHER VARIETY *A. macrorrhiza* 'Variegata' (variegated leaves marked creamy white, grey-green or dark green).

PLANT PROFILE	
HEIGHT 2.4m (8ft)	
SPREAD 1.2m (4ft)	
SITE Filtered light	
SOIL Equal parts composted bark, loam and sand	
HARDINESS Min 15–18°C (59–64°F)	
FLOWERING Summer	

A | *Ananas comosus* var. *variegatus* Pineapple

WITH PLENTY OF LUCK you might be able to pick your own, not necessarily tasty, pineapples from *A comosus* var. *variegatus*, which has a dense rosette of spiny-edged leaves with attractive yellowish-white stripes. It grows in the wild in Brazil, where it produces violet-blue or purple flowers and reddish-yellow modified leaves at the base of the flower, followed by the bright red fruit that turns into the pineapples sold in shops. The plants need low to moderate humidity to fruit, and a draught-free position. Water freely in full growth, but slightly reduce watering and apply a weekly liquid feed as the fruit starts to swell; keep barely moist at other times.

OTHER VARIETIES *A. bracteatus* 'Tricolor' (green leaves with yellow stripes – *see inset*); *A. comosus* (without the leaf stripes).

PLANT PROFILE
HEIGHT 1m (3ft)
SPREAD 50cm (20in)
SITE Full light
SOIL Terrestrial bromeliad compost
HARDINESS Min 15°C (59°F)
FLOWERING Summer

Anigozanthos flavidus Kangaroo paw

A

PLANT PROFILE

AN EVERGREEN FROM WESTERN AUSTRALIA, the kangaroo paw (or cat's paw) gets its name from the claw-like look of the woolly, yellow-green to brownish-red flowers that grow on its long stems (*see inset*). In the wild, the plant makes a bushy clump up to 3m (10ft) high, but in a pot, its narrow olive to mid-green leaves grow about 35cm (14in) long. If planted outside in a summer border, it needs rich, moist but free-draining soil, but the roots may need a trim before it is packed back into a conservatory pot for winter. Water freely with rain- or soft water when in full growth, provide a monthly liquid feed in summer, and water sparingly in winter.

OTHER VARIETY *A. manglesii* (the mangles' kangaroo paw has yellow-green flowers and grows about 90cm/3ft high).

HEIGHT 1.2m (4ft)	
SPREAD 45cm (18in)	
SITE Bright filtered light	
SOIL 3 parts leafmould to 1 part loam and sharp sand	
HARDINESS Min 5°C (41°F)	
FLOWERING Late spring to midsummer	

A

Anthurium crystallinum Flamingo flower

THIS SOUTH AMERICAN, TROPICAL PLANT has fabulous leaves that grow 30–45cm (12–18in) long and have a velvety rich green colour with an array of distinctive white veins. Although its greenish-yellow flower-like structures would look stunning outside in a summer border, it must remain in a warm humid conservatory. An epiphytic plant (one which grows on a host plant), it is usually sold attached to a moss pole. If in a pot, replace the top layer of soil every spring, and repot every two years. Water well when in full growth, giving a liquid feed every two to three weeks. Water sparingly in winter, when less humid conditions are required.

OTHER VARIETIES *A. andraeanum* (red 'flowers'); *A. scherzerianum* (glossy leaves with bright red 'flowers').

PLANT PROFILE
HEIGHT 60cm (24in)
SPREAD 60cm (24in)
SITE Filtered summer sun; full winter sun
SOIL Free-draining; 1 part loam, 2–3 parts leafmould
HARDINESS Min 16°C (61°F)
FLOWERING Intermittently

Anthurium scherzerianum

A

WORTH GROWING FOR ITS LEAVES AND 'FLOWERS', *A. scherzerianum* is tricky to keep because it needs plenty of warmth and humidity. In the right conditions, it produces 15–21cm (6–8in) long, glossy dark green leaves and, intermittently throughout the year, strange, orange-red flower-like structures. It is often sold attached to a mossy pole because it is epiphytic (grows on a host plant) in the wild. Repot every two years and replace the top layer of soil every spring if in a pot. Water well in full growth, providing a liquid feed every two to three weeks; reduce watering in winter, when less humidity is required. Protect against mealybugs and scale insects.

OTHER VARIETIES *A. andraeanum* (red 'flowers'); *A. crystallinum* (rich green, white-veined leaves, green-yellow 'flowers').

PLANT PROFILE
HEIGHT To 60cm (24in)
SPREAD To 60cm (24in)
SITE Filtered summer sun; full winter sun
SOIL Free-draining; 1 part loam, 2–3 parts leafmould
HARDINESS Min 16°C (61°F)
FLOWERING Intermittently

A | *Aphelandra squarrosa* 'Dania' **Saffron-spike**

THE LEAVES OF THIS BRAZILIAN PLANT, also known as a zebra plant, are its main feature. The glossy, leathery, dark green foliage has dramatic, bright white veins, and each leaf grows up to 20cm (8in) long. The rare yellow or orange-yellow flower-like structures – if they appear – create an extraordinary contrast. Warm and humid conditions are essential, as is compost with additions of leafmould. Give moderate drinks of rainwater when in full growth, adding a liquid feed every two weeks; water more sparingly in winter. Mist leaves frequently, and cut back straggly growth in early spring or autumn. Aphelandras are susceptible to aphid attacks.

OTHER VARIETY *A. squarrosa* 'Louisae' (equally dramatic leaves with red-tipped, golden-yellow 'flowers').

PLANT PROFILE
HEIGHT 60cm (24in)
SPREAD 45cm (18in)
SITE Filtered summer light; full winter light
SOIL 3 parts John Innes No. 2 to 1 part leafmould
HARDINESS Min 7°C (45°F)
FLOWERING Late summer and autumn

Aporocactus flagelliformis Rat's tail cactus

RAT'S TAIL PERFECTLY DESCRIBES the long, thin, greyish-green spiny stems of this fast-growing cactus. Over an eight-week period from late spring, the dangling stems are partly covered with flashy purple-red flowers that are about 8cm (3in) long. In its native Mexico, it grows in trees and among rocks, but in the conservatory it needs to be kept in a hanging basket out of direct, burning sun. Water moderately over summer, giving it a monthly, liquid tomato feed until all the flowers have faded; keep just moist throughout the rest of the year, particularly in winter. Mealybugs may be a problem.

PLANT PROFILE
HEIGHT 10cm (4in)
SPREAD 90cm (3ft)
SITE Bright filtered light
SOIL Epiphytic compost
HARDINESS Min 7°C (45°F)
FLOWERING Late spring to early summer

A *Araucaria heterophylla* Norfolk Island pine

A HIGHLY ATTRACTIVE EVERGREEN CONIFER, the Norfolk Island
pine has stiff branches that are nicely tiered, with bright, light green
needles. In its native Norfolk Island, in the Pacific Ocean, it may hit
45m (150ft), but in a conservatory pot (*see inset*), it will take several
years to grow to 2.5m (8ft). At this point, it will probably
need replacing by a younger plant. Water freely in summer, giving a
liquid feed every two weeks, when it may also be placed outside in
dappled shade. Keep just moist in winter. If the needles turn yellow
and fall off, it means that the conservatory is too warm and dry.

PLANT PROFILE
HEIGHT 2–2.5m (6–8ft)
SPREAD 1.2–1.5m (4–5ft)
SITE Bright sun
SOIL John Innes No. 2
HARDINESS Min 4°C (39°F)

Araujia sericifera Cruel plant

A

THIS TWINING EVERGREEN CLIMBER needs plenty of space to grow and may reach 10m (30ft) in its native South America. Although it is far more modest in a conservatory pot, growing to just half that height, it will need a framework of wires fitted to a large wall. From late summer to autumn, the cruel plant produces an abundance of scented white or pale pink flowers, which are extremely sticky at their base (the common name refers to the fact that moths become trapped in this sticky pollen). Water moderately over summer, providing a monthly liquid feed; give a sparing drink in winter. Protect against red spider mites.

PLANT PROFILE

HEIGHT 4.5m (13½ft)

SPREAD 2m (6ft)

SITE Full light

SOIL John Innes No. 2

HARDINESS Half hardy

FLOWERING Late summer to autumn

Ardisia crenata

THE BRIGHT RED BERRIES in late autumn are the key attraction of *A. crenata*, and make a good show against the glossy, dark green leaves (*see inset*). The berries are preceded by the small white or pink summer flowers, which are best pollinated by hand using a small, soft paint brush. Give a light, early spring prune for shape, and to promote vigorous new growth. Water freely when in full growth, giving a monthly liquid feed; provide a moderate drink at other times. If the flowers fall off without producing berries, the plant needs to be moved out of a draught. Red spider mites and mealybugs may be a problem.

PLANT PROFILE

HEIGHT 90cm (3ft)	
SPREAD 60cm (24in)	
SITE Bright light	
SOIL John Innes No. 2	
HARDINESS Min 10°C (50°F)	
FLOWERING Summer	

Aristolochia littoralis Calico Flower

A WEIRD AND WACKY CLIMBER, it has small flowers like a curved, baroque smoker's pipe with a U-bend in the middle. Although the flared lips are attractively mottled purple-brown and white, they tend to get hidden amongst the plant's heart-shaped, deciduous leaves and twisting, twining stems. To help show off the flowers, grow the plant up horizontal wires set against a conservatory wall. Note that the calico flower must endure a chilly winter period before any new growth will begin. Water freely in full growth, giving a monthly liquid feed; water sparingly in winter.

OTHER VARIETIES *A. gigantea* (large maroon and white flowers); *A. grandiflora* (huge flowers, needs warm conditions).

PLANT PROFILE

HEIGHT 1.8m (6ft)

SPREAD 1.8m (6ft)

SITE Bright filtered light

SOIL Loamless potting compost

HARDINESS Min 7°C (45°F)

FLOWERING Summer

A *Asparagus setaceus* 'Nanus'

WITH ITS ARCHING STEMS and delicate feathery foliage, 'Nanus' is
the ideal fern for a small space, and looks particularly good in a
stylish white room when it is picked up by an adjacent light. It is
also very easy to look after, as long as you keep it out of direct
summer sun and water freely from early spring to mid-autumn,
applying a monthly liquid feed; water sparingly over winter. Do not
confuse 'Nanus' with its South African parent, *A. setaceus* – this is a
very different plant, a bushy climber that can reach up to 2.5m (8ft).
'Nanus' is susceptible to red spider mites and scale insects.

PLANT PROFILE

HEIGHT	45cm (18in)
SPREAD	45cm (18in)
SITE	Bright filtered light
SOIL	John Innes No. 2
HARDINESS	Half hardy
FLOWERING	Summer

Aspidistra elatior 'Variegata' Cast-iron plant

A

A BIG FAVOURITE IN VICTORIAN TIMES, when it was grown in parlours and prized because it could withstand poor conditions, the cast-iron plant has given rise to this form with variegated leaves. Some plants have creamy-white stripes or wider bands along the leaf edges and down the leaf stalks; on older leaves, the variegated areas may turn brown in bright light. Grow it as a feature plant in a special place, and for its cream-coloured flowers. Water moderately when in full growth, but sparingly over winter. Once the cast-iron plant is established, apply a monthly liquid feed. Mealybugs and red spider mites may be a problem.

OTHER VARIETY *A. elatior* (glossy, dark green leaves); *A. elatior* 'Milky Way' (spotted leaves – *see inset*).

PLANT PROFILE	
HEIGHT To 60cm (24in)	
SPREAD To 60cm (24in)	
SITE Bright filtered light	
SOIL John Innes No. 2	
HARDINESS Frost hardy	
FLOWERING Early summer	

Asplenium nidus Bird's-nest fern

A HIGHLY DISTINCTIVE, EASY-GOING, evergreen foliage plant, the bird's nest fern has a clustered group of glossy, bright green leaves with a distinctive central vein. In the wilds of moist, tropical Asia, the plant is found growing among tree branches, but it can be grown in a conservatory pot in warm, humid conditions (*see inset*). Keep out of direct sun or the leaves will burn. When it is growing well, new leaves will unfurl upwards out of the clustered growth. Water moderately when in growth, adding a monthly, half-strength liquid feed; water sparingly in winter. Keep out of draughts and protect against scale insects.

OTHER VARIETY *A. bulbiferum* (dark green leaves).

PLANT PROFILE

HEIGHT 90cm (3ft)

SPREAD 90cm (3ft)

SITE Bright filtered light

SOIL Equal parts loam, leafmould (or peat substitute) and sharp sand

HARDINESS Min 10°C (50°F)

Astrophytum myriostigma Bishop's cap

THIS TINY, SLOW-GROWING MEXICAN CACTUS has a squat and toad-like, often five-sided shape, but after many years will look more like a column. The skin or body of the bishop's cap is green, blue or purple, and its scores of tiny white dots are actually crude, miniscule spines. The yellow, often red-centred, flowers only last a few days, but they are followed by more. It is slightly trickier than most cacti – be sure to water it moderately over the growing season, adding a low-nitrogen liquid feed, and keep it dry when dormant in winter. The quickest way to kill it is by overwatering. Beware mealybugs.

OTHER VARIETIES *A. asterias* (resembles a sea urchin); *A. ornatum* (small, squat, eight-ribbed cactus with vicious spines).

PLANT PROFILE	
HEIGHT 15cm (6in)	
SPREAD 20cm (8in)	
SITE Bright filtered light	
SOIL Cactus compost with added limestone chippings	
HARDINESS Min 10°C (50°F)	
FLOWERING Summer	

B

Begonia 'Batik'

THERE ARE THOUSANDS OF FIRST-RATE BEGONIAS, which range in size from midgets to giants and are grown for their brightly-coloured leaves and/or attractive flowers. 'Batik' has an extremely impressive cluster of double apricot-pink flowers set above the glossy leaves, which makes a compact show from late autumn to early spring (*see inset*). Provide filtered light on warm sunny days, and move to a cooler place if the temperature exceeds 19°C (66°F). In summer, water only when the compost has dried out, adding a half-strength liquid feed each time; water sparingly in winter. Protect against pests and diseases, from aphids to powdery mildew.

OTHER VARIETIES *B.* 'Munchkin' (pink flowers and bronze leaves); *B.* 'Nora Bedson' (pink flowers, mottled leaves).

PLANT PROFILE
HEIGHT 23cm (9in)
SPREAD 20cm (8in)
SITE Bright light
SOIL John Innes No. 2
HARDINESS Min 10°C (50°F)
FLOWERING Winter

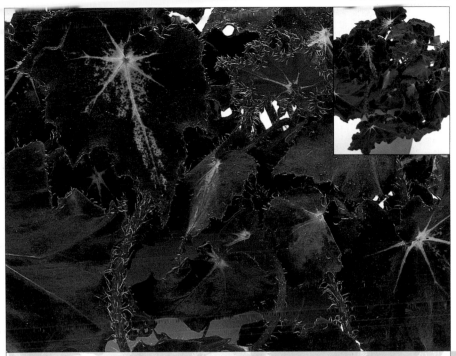

Begonia 'Beatrice Haddrell'

B

THE SELLING POINT of 'Beatrice Haddrell' is the foliage – near star-shaped, almost black leaves with bright green veins, which make a nice contrast against the light pink flowers. When placed amongst a group of pot plants (*see inset*), it will also help to set off any adjacent white or yellow flowers. Provide filtered light when the sun is strong, and move to a cooler place if the temperature exceeds 19°C (66°F). Add a half-strength liquid feed to each watering in the summer months, but do this only once the compost has dried out; water sparingly in winter. Begonias are prone to various pests and diseases, including aphids and powdery mildew.

OTHER VARIETIES *B.* 'Bethlehem Star' (black-green leaves); *B.* 'Enech' (near-black leaves).

PLANT PROFILE	
HEIGHT 20cm (8in)	
SPREAD 22cm (9in)	
SITE Bright light	
SOIL John Innes No. 2	
HARDINESS Min 10°C (50°F)	
FLOWERING Winter	

B *Begonia bowerae* Eyelash begonia

THIS BEGONIA'S 'EYELASHES' are actually the tiny white hairs that appear along the margins of its attractive leaves, which are bright green with chocolate brown markings. Its clusters of white flowers are held well above the foliage. Shield begonias from hot sun by placing in filtered light, and moving them to a cooler place if the temperature exceeds 19°C (66°F). In summer, water only when the compost has dried out, adding a half-strength liquid feed each time; water sparingly in winter. Various pests and diseases, including mealybugs and thrips, may be a problem.

OTHER VARIETIES *B.* 'Cleopatra' (pale pink flowers, green with bronze-brown leaves); *B.* 'Tiger Paws' (small white flowers).

PLANT PROFILE
HEIGHT 25cm (10in)
SPREAD 18cm (7in)
SITE Bright light
SOIL John Innes No. 2
HARDINESS Min 10°C (50°F)
FLOWERING Winter to early spring

Begonia 'Irene Nuss'

B

THE CLUSTERS OF PINK FLOWERS on 'Irene Nuss' often appear well beyond summer (even into early winter), and they are nicely set off by the dark green-bronze leaves that are marked silvery pink. To prevent it from losing leaves low down, nip back the slender, bamboo-like stems in spring, leaving only two or three buds to create bushier growth. Avoid continuous direct sun, and move to a cooler place if the temperature exceeds 19°C (66°F). In summer, water only when the compost has dried out, and add a half-strength liquid feed; water sparingly in winter. Beware pests and diseases, especially aphids and powdery mildew.

OTHER VARIETY *B.* 'Orange Rubra' (a generous supply of orange and white flowers set against light green leaves with silver spots).

PLANT PROFILE
HEIGHT 75cm (30in)
SPREAD 60cm (24in)
SITE Bright light
SOIL John Innes No. 2
HARDINESS Min 10°C (50°F)
FLOWERING Summer to mid-autumn

B

Begonia listada

THIS SHRUBBY, COMPACT BRAZILIAN BEGONIA is popularly grown for its long narrow leaves, which resemble pouting, misshapen lips. They are dark green with an emerald green stripe on the upper surface and red underneath, and make a nice contrast with the white autumn/winter flowers. Provide filtered light on sunny days, and move to a cooler place if the temperature exceeds 19°C (66°F). In summer, water only when the compost has dried out, adding a half-strength liquid feed; water sparingly in winter. Begonias must be protected from a number of pests and diseases, including aphids and powdery mildew.

OTHER VARIETIES *B. fuchsioides* (red flowers resembling those of a fuchsia); *B.* 'Serlis' (slightly felted leaves).

PLANT PROFILE
HEIGHT 30cm (12in)
SPREAD 18cm (7in)
SITE Bright light
SOIL John Innes No. 2
HARDINESS Min 10°C (50°F)
FLOWERING Autumn to winter

Begonia masoniana Iron-cross begonia

B

THE HIGHLY DISTINCTIVE BLACK–BROWN MARK on this begonia's mid- to deep green leaves resembles the German Iron Cross. The rest of the 20cm (8in) long leaves are deep green and the flowers are greenish-white. The iron-cross begonia is notoriously tricky unless you can provide ideal conditions, including a humid conservatory atmosphere. Provide filtered light if the sun is hot, and move to a cooler place if the temperature reaches over 19°C (66°F). In summer, water only when the compost has dried out, adding a half-strength liquid feed each time; water sparingly in winter. Protect against pests and diseases, such as aphids and powdery mildew.

OTHER VARIETIES *B. rex* (green leaves with silver markings); *B. versicolor* (reddish-brown leaves with green and silver markings).

PLANT PROFILE
HEIGHT 50cm (20in)
SPREAD 45cm (18in)
SITE Bright light
SOIL John Innes No. 2
HARDINESS Min 10°C (50°F)
FLOWERING Summer

Begonia 'Merry Christmas'

THE EXTRAORDINARY, GLOSSY EVERGREEN LEAVES of this begonia are red in the centre and bright green around the edge. The pale rose-pink flowers appear in the last part of the year, from autumn until the start of winter. To maintain and deepen the red on the leaves, stand the plant in bright light, but move to a cooler place if the temperature exceeds 19°C (66°F). To avoid the risk of rotting, give it a drink by immersing the pot in a bucket of water in summer, but only once the compost has dried out, adding a half-strength liquid feed each time. In winter, water sparingly. Beware of pests and diseases, such as grey mould and stem rot.

OTHER VARIETY B. 'Pandora' (dark green leaves splashed pink and silver, pink flowers in the autumn).

PLANT PROFILE

HEIGHT 25cm (10in)

SPREAD 30cm (12in)

SITE Bright light

SOIL John Innes No. 2

HARDINESS Min 10°C (50°F)

FLOWERING Autumn to early winter

Begonia serratipetala

B

A SHRUB-LIKE BEGONIA from New Guinea, *B. serratipetala* has very striking, zig-zag-edged, reddish-brown pointy leaves that are about 8cm (3in) long and have raised pink spots. It is often grown in hanging baskets, where the leaves prove to be the plant's biggest asset – the small rose-pink flowers appear unpredictably and infrequently. Tricky to grow, but by no means impossible, it demands just the right amount of water. This basically means giving sparing drinks because too much or too little will cause the leaves to start dropping. It is also prone to a number of pests and diseases, including powdery mildew and aphids.

OTHER VARIETIES *B.* 'Ingramii' (shiny leaves, dark pink flowers); *B. luxurians* (often bronzish leaves, yellowish-white flowers).

PLANT PROFILE
HEIGHT 45cm (18in)
SPREAD 45cm (18in)
SITE Bright light
SOIL John Innes No. 2
HARDINESS Min 13°C (55°F)
FLOWERING Intermittently, all year

| B | *Billbergia* Fantasia Group Marbled rainbow plant |

A GOOD CHOICE FOR A COLLECTION of bromeliads, the Fantasia Group has the typical rosette of narrow leaves and eye-catching flowers. The lance-shaped, 30–45cm (12–18in) long leaves are copper-green with creamy-white and pink marbling, while the flowers are violet-blue at the top and red below. It is important that the central funnel is kept filled with rainwater or soft water: in the wild in its native Central and South America, moisture drips down constantly from the forest tree canopy. Water freely when in full growth, give a monthly liquid feed and spray plants once a week with soft water to provide humidity.

OTHER VARIETIES *B. nutans* (arching red-flushed stems with pale green flowers); *B.* x *windii* (long arching leaves, green flowers).

PLANT PROFILE

HEIGHT 50cm (20in)

SPREAD 45cm (18in)

SITE Bright indirect light

SOIL Epiphytic bromeliad compost

HARDINESS Min 10°C (50°F)

FLOWERING Summer

Blechnum gibbum

B

AN EVERGREEN FERN with terrific presence, *B. gibbum* has bright leaves (fronds) that may reach up to 2m (6ft) high in its native Fiji. It only grows about half as tall in a conservatory pot, and after a few years will resemble a miniature palm with a short trunk. It needs indirect light and decent humidity, which necessitates regular misting and good air ventilation. Beware a stagnant atmosphere, when the fronds soon discolour, as well as scorching caused by direct exposure to the hot summer sun. When standing it outside in hot weather, provide partial to deep shade, and place it next to a water feature to provide some humidity.

OTHER VARIETY *B. brasiliense* (similar, but with thinner fronds).

PLANT PROFILE

HEIGHT 90cm (3ft)

SPREAD 90cm (3ft)

SITE Bright filtered light

SOIL 1 part acid compost to 2 parts sharp sand and 3 parts leafmould

HARDINESS Min 18°C (64°F)

B

Bomarea caldasii

A SOUTH AMERICAN TWINING CLIMBER with slender stems, this bomarea is grown for its impressive clusters of up to 40 tubular flowers, which are brick-red to orange on the outside, and yellowish-green with red spots on the inside. If you have a mild inner city garden, *B. caldasii* can be grown in a sunny sheltered site on free-draining, fertile soil; otherwise, it needs to climb up a set of horizontal wires fixed to a conservatory wall where it will flower for longer. Water freely when in full growth, and apply a monthly liquid feed; keep just moist in winter. Cut back dead growth and any flowered stems to the ground in winter.

OTHER VARIETIES *B.cardieri* (large pink flowers, dark spots within); *B. hirtella* (green-orange flowers, orange inside).

PLANT PROFILE	
HEIGHT 1.8m (6ft)	
SPREAD 90cm (3ft)	
SITE Full light	
SOIL John Innes No. 3	
HARDINESS Half hardy	
FLOWERING Late spring to autumn	

Bougainvillea 'Scarlett O'Hara'

B

IN A MEDITERRANEAN GARDEN, 'Scarlett O' Hara' can easily hit 12m (40ft), but in a 30cm (12in) conservatory pot it will only grow to about 2m (6ft) high (taller in a conservatory border). Bougainvilleas can be a flamboyant choice, fun and brash, but note that what look like the flowers are actually colourful papery growths with the real flowers tucked away deep inside. Stand it outside over summer and prune the side-shoots in autumn, leaving three to four buds. Water freely when in growth, giving it a high–nitrogen feed, and provide a potash-rich feed when in bud. Keep just moist in winter. Beware red spider mites and mealybugs in a conservatory.

OTHER VARIETIES *B.* x *buttiana* 'Jamaica Red' (red 'flowers'); *B.* 'Raspberry Ice' (flashy, bright cerise 'flowers').

PLANT PROFILE	
HEIGHT 2m (6ft)	
SPREAD 2m (6ft)	
SITE Full light	
SOIL John Innes No. 3	
HARDINESS Min 4°C (39°F)	
FLOWERING Summer to autumn	

B *Browallia speciosa* 'White Troll' Sapphire Flower

BROWALLIAS ARE TROPICAL, South American perennials, 'White Troll' a compact form. Its flowers appear in clusters or alone, and are held just above the 10cm (4in) long, sometimes slightly sticky, leaves. To grow *B. speciosa* as an annual (which is discarded after flowering), sow seed in early spring for summer flowers, or in late summer for winter flowers. Pinch out the young growing tips for bushier, flowery growth. Provide good ventilation and protect it from direct scorching sun. Water moderately in full growth, with a monthly liquid feed; keep just moist in winter. Prone to aphids.

OTHER VARIETIES *B. speciosa* 'Blue Bells' (violet-blue flowers); *B. speciosa* 'Heavenly Bells' (sky-blue flowers); *B. speciosa* 'Silver Bells' (white flowers).

PLANT PROFILE	
HEIGHT To 25cm (10in)	
SPREAD 25cm (10in)	
SITE Full light	
SOIL John Innes No. 2	
HARDINESS Min 13–16°C (55–61°F)	
FLOWERING Summer	

Brugmansia x *candida* 'Grand Marnier' Angels' trumpet

B

SOMETIMES CALLED DATURA, this plant has superb, trumpet-shaped flowers that reach up to 30cm (12in) long and release a sweet scent in the evening. It also has dramatic, large, felt-like leaves. At the start of summer, place it in a border, in a sunny but sheltered position or strong winds will flay the leaves. Water well and give a tomato feed every two weeks from midsummer. Pot it up in a large container over winter, keeping it frost-free and barely watered. In spring, cut it back moderately or hard to a new shoot. If grown all year in a conservatory border, provide summer ventilation. Protect against red spider mites. All parts are toxic.

OTHER VARIETIES *B. arborea* (scented white flowers); *B.* x *candida* 'Knightii' (scented white flowers).

PLANT PROFILE	
HEIGHT 2.7m (9ft)	
SPREAD 1.8m (6ft)	
SITE Full sun	
SOIL John Innes No. 3	
HARDINESS Min 7°C (45°F)	
FLOWERING Midsummer to autumn	

B *Brunfelsia pauciflora* Yesterday, today and tomorrow

A FIRST-RATE SHRUB for the conservatory border or a pot, *B. pauciflora* is covered in a mass of flowers that change colour – they open purple, become mauve and fade to white on the third day (hence the common name). Although it will reach up to 3m (10ft) high in its native Brazil, it will not grow as big in a conservatory in northern Europe, and can be kept smaller and shapelier with a gentle to moderate prune after flowering. Pinch out young plants to create bushier, flowery growth. Water freely when in growth and give a liquid feed every three to four weeks; water sparingly over winter. Beware red spider mites and mealybugs.

OTHER VARIETY *B. pauciflora* 'Floribunda' (smaller, with flowers changing from violet to purple).

PLANT PROFILE

HEIGHT 1–1.5m (3–5ft)

SPREAD 1–1.5m (3–5ft)

SITE Bright filtered light

SOIL John Innes No. 2

HARDINESS Min 7°C (45°F)

FLOWERING Spring to summer

Caladium bicolor 'Pink Beauty' Angel wings

CALADIUMS ARE GROWN for their superb, heart-shaped, exquisitely-coloured leaves, which range from rich red with green edging to white with red splashes. 'Pink Beauty' has red-veined leaves that are pink in the centre with speckled bright green margins. The parent plant, *C. bicolor*, comes from South America, and it is essential to recreate these tropical conditions – provide high humidity over summer and a draught-free position. Water freely and apply a monthly liquid feed, but reduce the amount of water in the autumn. Keep almost dry (give it just enough water to prevent drying out) at 13–16°C (55–61°F) when dormant over winter.

OTHER VARIETIES *C. bicolor* 'June Bride' (silvery-white leaves with green veins); *C.* 'Freida Hemple' (red leaves, green edging).

PLANT PROFILE
HEIGHT 30cm (12in)
SPREAD 30cm (12in)
SITE Bright filtered light
SOIL Loamless potting compost
HARDINESS Min 13°C (55°F)
FLOWERING Spring

Calathea crocata

THE TROPICAL CALATHEAS are grown mainly for their astonishing leaves, many of which are beautifully patterned, but *C. crocata* has the added advantage of superb flowers. The upward-pointing, bright orange blooms contrast nicely with the dusky, dark green leaves that are purple beneath. Note that it needs hothouse conditions, especially to flower, and must be kept it in a draught-free, humid position at a constant temperature. Avoid direct light, which will scorch the leaves. Water freely in full growth and apply a monthly liquid feed; water moderately over winter. Aphids and red spider mites may be a problem.

OTHER VARIETIES *C. majestica* (striped dark green leaves); *C. makoyana* (pale green with green lines and dark patches).

PLANT PROFILE

HEIGHT 30cm (12in)

SPREAD 30cm (12in))

SITE Filtered light

SOIL John Innes No. 2

HARDINESS Min 16–21°C (61–70°F)

FLOWERING Summer

Calathea zebrina Zebra plant

THIS EXCEPTIONAL, VELVETY FOLIAGE PLANT is grown for its 45cm (18in) long, oval, beautifully-patterned leaves that are banded dark and light green on the upper surface and are red underneath. Each leaf is nicely held out on a 30cm (12in) long stalk. Like other calatheas, it needs pampering – always keep it in a draught-free, humid position (out of direct light, which can scorch the leaves) and at a constant temperature. Water freely when in full growth, provide a monthly liquid feed and then water moderately over the winter period. Susceptible to aphids and red spider mites.

OTHER VARIETIES *C. picturata* 'Argentea' (leaves are silvery-white above, rich purple beneath); *C. roseopicta* (dark green leaves with pink or cream stripes).

PLANT PROFILE
HEIGHT 60cm (24in)
SPREAD 60cm (24in)
SITE Filtered light
SOIL John Innes No. 2
HARDINESS Min 16–21°C (61–70°F)
FLOWERING Summer

C | *Calceolaria* 'Walter Shrimpton' **Slipper flower**

THE WONDERFULLY ECCENTRIC 'WALTER SHRIMPTON' produces bizarre, bronze-yellow flowers with a horizontal white band half-way up, and a heavy concentration of rich-brown speckling at the bottom. It might look as if it needs hothouse conditions and pampering, but it is surprisingly easy to grow and should be kept in a cool environment. Provide good ventilation over the growing period, and keep it out of direct light. Water freely over summer, keeping the soil moist at all times, and apply a liquid feed every three to four weeks; water sparingly over winter. Protect against aphids and red spider mites.

OTHER VARIETY *C.* Herbeohybrida Group (blotched, pouch-like spring flowers that appear in a range of bright colours).

PLANT PROFILE
HEIGHT 10cm (4in)
SPREAD 23cm (9in)
SITE Bright filtered light
SOIL John Innes No. 2
HARDINESS Fully hardy
FLOWERING Summer

Calliandra haematocephala Powder-puff tree

C

AN EXCEPTIONAL EVERGREEN CONSERVATORY PLANT, the powder-puff tree makes a lovely show right through the year. The foliage consists of five to ten leaflets that have a pink tinge when young. The winter flowers, which are usually red but may be pink or white (*see inset*), are about 6.5cm (2½in) wide. They are a real boon with their fluffy powder-puff look, and although short-lived, are replaced by a regular supply of buds. Prune for space after flowering. In the summer, be sure to shade from the hot sun and provide some humidity. Water well from early summer to autumn and add a monthly liquid feed; reduce watering over winter. Red spider mites and scale insects may be a problem.

PLANT PROFILE
HEIGHT 1.8m (6ft)
SPREAD 1.2m (4ft)
SITE Full light
SOIL John Innes No. 2
HARDINESS Min 13°C (55°F)
FLOWERING Winter

C

Callisia repens

THIS SOUTH AMERICAN TRAILING PERENNIAL has dangling stems that can grow down over the side of a hanging basket to a length of 60cm (2ft). The leaves are small, round and apple green, while the autumn flowers are white. *C. repens* can get a bit straggly – nip back the stems in spring to make it bushier and more compact (*see inset*). Do not move it into a larger pot unless the roots are trying to burst out of its current container. Bright light is important, but avoid scorching summer sun. Water moderately in full growth, adding a monthly liquid feed; give a sparing drink over winter. New plants are easily raised from 7cm (3in) long cuttings taken in the spring.

OTHER VARIETIES *C. elegans* (white-striped, olive-green leaves, purple beneath); *C. navicularis* (copper-green leaves, purple beneath).

PLANT PROFILE

HEIGHT 15cm (6in)

SPREAD 23cm (9in)

SITE Bright filtered light

SOIL 2 parts John Innes No. 2 to 1 part coarse grit

HARDINESS Min 10°C (50°F)

FLOWERING Autumn

Camellia japonica 'Lovelight' Common camellia

C

A SUBSTANTIAL, VIGOROUS, UPRIGHT CAMELLIA, 'Lovelight' is a superb plant for a conservatory border or tub, where it can reach about 2.7m (9ft) high – its parent plant, *C. japonica*, grows three times this height in the Far East. 'Lovelight' has large leaves and produces white flowers with a dash of yellow in the middle. Like all camellias, it needs ericaceous (lime-free) compost. When watering, use rain- or soft water, and apply a monthly liquid feed from mid-spring to early summer. Spray for humidity in winter, and keep the temperature constant when in bud or the leaves will drop. In a pot, it may stay outside over summer in a partially shaded, sheltered site.

OTHER VARIETIES *C. japonica* 'Berenice Boddy' (pink flowers); *C. japonica* 'Mars' (red flowers); *C. japonica* 'Nuccios Jewel' (white flowers).

PLANT PROFILE
HEIGHT 2.7m (9ft)
SPREAD 1.5m (5ft)
SITE Bright filtered light
SOIL Ericaceous
HARDINESS Fully hardy
FLOWERING Midwinter to mid-spring

C | *Campanula isophylla* Italian bellflower

AN EXCELLENT PLANT for a pot or hanging basket, the Italian bellflower has soft stems topped by pale blue or white flowers that bloom over a long period. It can be grown on its own as a summery feature plant or in a mix with brightly-coloured annuals. If placed outside in summer, bring indoors in early autumn to avoid the cold and wet; provide good ventilation if it is grown inside. After its flowering season, when the plant becomes dormant, cut back dead stems to the base; new growth will appear next spring. Water moderately in full growth and apply a monthly liquid feed; keep moist in winter. Beware aphids and red spider mites.

OTHER VARIETY *C. isophylla* 'Alba' (large white flowers); *C. isophylla* Kristal hybrids (blue and white flowers).

PLANT PROFILE
HEIGHT 15–20cm (6–8in)
SPREAD To 30cm (12in)
SITE Bright filtered light
SOIL John Innes No. 2
HARDINESS Half hardy
FLOWERING Summer to autumn

Canarina canariensis Canary bellflower

THIS MINIATURE, SCRAMBLING, DECIDUOUS CLIMBER adds an exuberant and colourful touch to a winter conservatory. The bell-shaped flowers are flashy orange-red to orange-yellow with attractive veins and are usually about 5cm (2in) long. Growth starts in late summer, when it needs horizontal wall wires for the stems to weave through and cling on to; it dies down again the following spring. Provide bright light and water well when in full growth, adding a liquid feed every two to three weeks. After the leaves have turned yellow and dropped in the spring, keep the plant dry over summer while dormant. Start gently watering again in about three months, when new growth begins.

PLANT PROFILE

HEIGHT 1m (3ft)

SPREAD 75cm (30in)

SITE Bright filtered light

SOIL John Innes No. 3

HARDINESS Min 5°C (41°F)

FLOWERING Winter to spring

C | *Canna* 'King Midas' Indian shot plant

CANNAS HAVE A LUSH, TROPICAL AIR and are surprisingly easy to grow. 'King Midas' sends up a vertical stem topped by golden-yellow flowers with orange markings (similar to those of a gladiolus). The blooms, which sit just above the large, green paddle-like leaves, make a striking contrast. It takes up plenty of space – keep the front of it clear for maximum impact – and is best grown in a conservatory or greenhouse border because the underground portions tend to spread and send up new stems. Water freely when in full growth, and apply a monthly liquid tomato feed. Cut off the top growth in late autumn, and keep dry while dormant over winter.

OTHER VARIETIES   *C.* 'Striata' (yellow-green leaves with yellow veins, orange flowers); *C.* 'Wyoming' (dark leaves, orange flowers).

PLANT PROFILE
HEIGHT 1.5m (5ft)
SPREAD 50cm (20in)
SITE Full light
SOIL Loamless potting compost
HARDINESS Half hardy
FLOWERING Midsummer to early autumn

Capsicum annuum 'Festival' Ornamental pepper

BRIGHT AND CHEERY, this pepper is grown for its sweet-shop effect of multi-coloured fruit (but warn children they are much too hot to eat). Nip out the tips of the young plant before the flower buds appear to make it even bushier and with more fruit. Keep 'Festival' out of direct sun, mist to keep it humid in dry conditions, and water when the surface of the compost is just dry. Add a liquid feed every two weeks (alternate a general-purpose feed with a tomato one). 'Festival' is generally sold as a winter-flowering pot plant, after which it may be discarded. To grow summer peppers for salads, and hot peppers, contact a specialist nursery or seed supplier.

OTHER VARIETIES *C. annuum* (the smaller Chilli pepper has red or yellow fruit); C. *annuum* 'Carnival Red' (orange-red fruit).

PLANT PROFILE
HEIGHT 60cm (2ft)
SPREAD 60cm (2ft)
SITE Bright sun
SOIL John Innes No. 2
HARDINESS Min 4°C (39°F)
FLOWERING Winter

C | *Caryota mitis* Burmese fish-tail palm

A PALM WITH QUITE A DIFFERENCE, the Burmese fish-tail palm
produces a clump of stems with long, rich green leaves consisting
of up to 60 leaflets. In its native south-east Asia, Burma and the
Philippines, it can reach 12m (40ft) high, but it is much more
restrained in a conservatory border where it grows about as high
as a house door (*see inset*). It needs high humidity levels, plenty of
water and a monthly liquid feed when in full growth. Be sparing
with winter drinks. For the best choice, hunt down a specialist
nursery. Vulnerable to red spider mites.

OTHER VARIETIES *C. ochlandra* (slightly white trunk with triangular
leaves); *C. maxima* (long triangular leaves); *C. urens* (the sago palm has a
single stem and arching dark green leaves).

PLANT PROFILE

HEIGHT 2m (6ft)

SPREAD 1.2m (4ft)

SITE Bright filtered light

SOIL John Innes No. 3

HARDINESS Min 15°C
(59°F)

FLOWERING Summer

Catharanthus roseus Madagascar periwinkle

C

AN EXTREMELY ATTRACTIVE EVERGREEN, Madagascar periwinkle forms a small clump (given space in a conservatory border) of glossy, dark green leaves with pink, rose-pink, red or white flowers. If grown in a pot, it can be stood outside over summer. In late winter, move it into a slightly larger pot or replace the top layer of soil. Because new plants have the best display of flowers, it may need to be replaced every two years. Good ventilation is important, as is moderate watering over summer, when it also needs a monthly liquid feed. Prone to red spider mites and whiteflies. Madagascar periwinkle is toxic if ingested.

OTHER VARIETIES *C. roseus* Cooler Series (compact and branching); *C. roseus* Ocellatus Group (red-eyed flowers).

PLANT PROFILE	
HEIGHT 30cm (12in)	
SPREAD 30cm (12in)	
SITE Full light	
SOIL John Innes No. 2	
HARDINESS Min 5–7°C (41–45°F)	
FLOWERING Spring to summer	

C

Cattleya bowringiana

YOU DO NOT NEED TO BE A BOTANIST with a high-tech conservatory to grow orchids. This flashy, waxy, rose to magenta flowering plant with a white throat comes from Guatemala, where it grows on the stems of other plants, but it will thrive in a conservatory pot. It needs high humidity, good ventilation and bright light (but not scorching sun – avoid windowsills in summer). Keep the temperature below 30°C (86°F). Water freely over summer, adding a liquid feed every third watering. In winter, remove any shading and water much more sparingly. Beware various pests, including red spider mites, aphids and mealybugs.

OTHER VARIETIES *C. bicolor* 'Chocolate Drop' (chocolate-brown to reddish-orange flowers); *C. walkeriana* (amethyst or white flowers).

PLANT PROFILE
HEIGHT 53cm (21in)
SPREAD 25cm (10in)
SITE Bright light
SOIL Epiphytic orchid compost
HARDINESS Min 5°C (41°F)
FLOWERING Autumn to winter

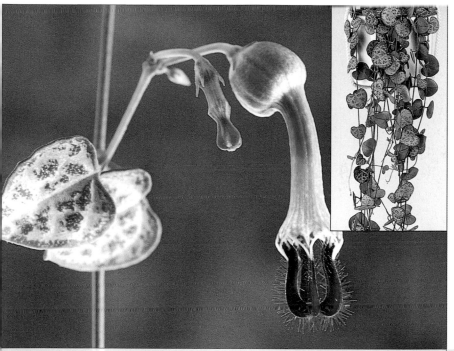

Ceropegia linearis subsp. *woodii* Hearts on a string

C

AN EASILY-GROWN SUCCULENT, hearts on a string needs to be grown
in a hanging basket (*see inset*) to show off its extraordinary long
trailing stems, each with small, attractive heart-shaped leaves at
intervals down its length. The leaves are typically green and silver,
and purple beneath, but both the shape and the colours on the top
side may vary. The mauve-pink flowers open in summer and are
followed by twin-horned seed pods. Water moderately when in full
growth, giving a diluted nitrogen liquid feed two to three times in
all; keep dry at other times. Avoid overwatering and low
temperatures, which can be fatal. Susceptible to aphids.

OTHER VARIETY *C. sandersonii* (cone-shaped flowers with
parachute-like canopy; a massive spreader).

PLANT PROFILE
HEIGHT 10cm (4in)
SPREAD About 1.8m (6ft)
SITE Bright filtered light
SOIL 2 parts sharp sand to 1 part compost, peat substitute and leafmould
HARDINESS Min 10°C (50°F)
FLOWERING Summer

C | *Cestrum elegans*

THE TALL, ARCHING GROWTH of this cestrum means that it is best grown against a conservatory wall and trained along strong horizontal wires to give support and ensure that the clusters of purple-red (or sometimes pink) flowers are well displayed. The shiny purple-red berries and downy evergreen leaves are added attractions. It is important to shade *C. elegans* from hot sun and provide some ventilation. Water moderately in full growth and apply a monthly liquid feed; water sparingly in winter. Give a light trim if necessary in mid- or late spring to create a balanced shape. Heavy pruning can restrict its size, but not by much.

OTHER VARIETY *C.* 'Newellii' (dark green, evergreen leaves and crimson summer flowers followed by berries).

PLANT PROFILE
HEIGHT 3m (10ft)
SPREAD 2.4m (8ft)
SITE Full light
SOIL John Innes No. 3
HARDINESS Min 5°C (41°F)
FLOWERING Summer to autumn

Cestrum parqui Willow-leaved jessamine

C

THIS SOUTH AMERICAN DECIDUOUS SHRUB has bright yellow-green tubular flowers (followed by berries) that release enough gorgeous scent in the evenings to fill a conservatory. Do not try growing it in a pot; instead, place it in a border against a wall with horizontal wires for it to ramble through, or against a vertical post for it to circle around. Shade from hot sun and water moderately when in growth, applying a monthly liquid feed; water sparingly in winter. Prune hard in early spring to keep it under control, and cut back flowered stems close to the soil.

OTHER VARIETY   *C. aurantiacum* (clusters of bright orange flowers).

PLANT PROFILE
HEIGHT 1.2m (4ft)
SPREAD 1.2m (4ft)
SITE Full light
SOIL John Innes No. 3
HARDINESS Frost hardy
FLOWERING Summer to autumn

C *Chamaedorea elegans* **Parlour palm**

THIS ELEGANT, MEXICAN RAINFOREST PALM makes a good choice for a conservatory. It is slow growing and has several slender, vertical stems that arch up out of the soil and are topped by long, thin, rich green leaves. Mature plants might flower when a reddish–yellow stem appears, sometimes producing tiny yellow-orange flowers that initially look like berries, but they are not a key feature. Mist in dry conditions to create some humidity. Provide filtered or indirect light and water freely when in full growth, giving a monthly liquid feed; water sparingly over winter. Protect against red spider mites.

OTHER VARIETIES *C. metallica* (one stem, topped by leaves); *C. microspadix* (group of stems, blue-green leaves).

PLANT PROFILE
HEIGHT 1.8m (6ft)
SPREAD 1m (3ft)
SITE Bright filtered light
SOIL 2 parts John Innes No. 2 to 1 part peat substitute
HARDINESS Min 16°C (61°F)
FLOWERING Summer

Chamelaucium uncinatum 'Album'   Geraldton wax

AN EVERGREEN SHRUB from western Australia, 'Album' has dark green leaves with clusters of pure white flowers that are good for cutting. In the wild, it grows on sandy heathland and seasonally dry scrub, which means that in a conservatory border it needs ericaceous (lime-free) soil. Alternatively, grow it in a pot and stand in the garden over summer at the foot of a sunny wall so that it does not get too much rain. Water moderately when in growth, and apply a monthly liquid feed to well-established plants. Lightly prune after flowering for shape and space.

OTHER VARIETY *C. uncinatum* (purple, mauve, red, pink or white flowers).

PLANT PROFILE
HEIGHT 2m (6ft)
SPREAD 1.2m (4ft))
SITE Full light
SOIL Ericaceous
HARDINESS Half hardy (borderline)
FLOWERING Spring to summer

C | *Chamaerops humilis* Dwarf fan palm

FOUND IN THE WILD on rocky, sandy slopes in the western Mediterranean, this miniature palm is worth growing for its splendid, splayed, fan-like leaves consisting of 12 to 15 fingers (*see inset*). The yellow flowers are extremely rare. Being half hardy, it can be planted outside when it gets too big for a conservatory, but this is only possible in the mildest, frost-free, sheltered gardens, and where the soil is poor and free-draining. If being grown in a conservatory pot, move the palm into a slightly larger container in the spring, or replace the top layer of soil. It needs moderate watering in full growth, and a monthly liquid feed; water sparingly in winter. Red spider mites can be a problem if being kept indoors.

PLANT PROFILE
HEIGHT 1.4m (5ft)
SPREAD 1.4m (5ft)
SITE Full to bright indirect light
SOIL John Innes No. 3
HARDINESS Half hardy
FLOWERING Summer

Chlorophytum comosum 'Vittatum'   **Spider plant**

C

THE DANGLING UMBILICAL CORDS of an established spider plant, with its young plants at the end like circling satellites, is an astonishing sight, especially when placed in a hanging basket in the centre of a room. The young plants, easily snipped off in the spring to be raised in small pots filled with cuttings compost, quickly produce a mass of long, thin, arching leaves that are striped green and white. The sprays of small summer flowers add an airy look. This plant is extremely easy to look after – shade from hot sun and water freely when in full growth, moderately at other times. Give a liquid feed every two weeks over summer.

OTHER VARIETIES *C. comosum* (all-green leaves); *C. comosum* 'Variegatum' (green leaves with white central stripes).

PLANT PROFILE
HEIGHT 20–25cm (8–10in)
SPREAD Up to 35cm (14in)
SITE Bright indirect to full light
SOIL John Innes No. 2
HARDINESS Min 7°C (45°F)
FLOWERING Spring and summer

C

Chrysalidocarpus lutescens Areca palm

AN IMPRESSIVE MADAGASCAN PALM, also known as the butterfly palm or the golden feather palm, it has a small clump of green and gold bamboo-like stems that arch up, with a swathe of yellow-green foliage on top. The long, thin leaves create an open, graceful, fan-like look. Though growth is slow, the overall shape is striking. Each spring, it is important to replace the top layer of soil or move the plant into a slightly larger pot. Some humidity is essential because it will slowly die in a dry atmosphere. Shade from scorching sun and water freely when in full growth, giving a monthly liquid feed; water sparingly over winter. Protect against red spider mites and scale insects.

PLANT PROFILE
HEIGHT 2.4m (8ft)
SPREAD 1.8m (6ft)
SITE Bright filtered light
SOIL John Innes No. 3
HARDINESS Min 10–15°C (50–59°F)
FLOWERING Summer

Chrysanthemum 'George Griffiths'

CHRYSANTHEMUMS COME IN ALL SHAPES AND SIZES, from the small and daisy-like to the colourful, shaggy mopheads like 'George Griffiths'. Its mass of deep red tiny petals form a flowerhead that opens in early autumn and ends up about 14cm (5½in) wide. The trick is to nip off all the buds on each shoot except for the one at the end; with more energy going into it, the untouched flower will grow much larger. Given its height, it is best grown in a border with rich, slightly acid soil. Water regularly and give a liquid feed every week from midsummer until the buds begin to swell. Tie in the new growth to strong canes. Beware red spider mites and whiteflies.

OTHER VARIETIES *C.* 'Cherry Chintz' (cherry-red flowers); *C.* 'Patricia Millar' (pink flowers); *C.* 'Sam Oldham' (larger red flowers).

PLANT PROFILE
HEIGHT 1.3–1.5m (4½–5ft)
SPREAD 75cm (30in)
SITE Bright sun
SOIL Moist but well-drained, neutral to slightly acid
HARDINESS Half hardy
FLOWERING Early autumn

C

Cissus discolor

THE ELONGATED, HEART-SHAPED LEAVES are the main reason for growing the climbing *C. discolor*. They stick out from its thin, red stems, are about 15cm (6in) long and come in deep green with patches of silver, grey or pink, the undersides being maroon. The insignificant summer flowers are green with a red tint. Although growth is modest, *C. discolor* needs a group of canes to climb up so the leaves may be seen clearly. Prune for space in early spring. Water freely in full growth, applying a monthly liquid feed, with a sparing drink over winter. If growing in a pot, replace the top layer of soil each spring, or move into a larger pot. Prone to red spider mites.

OTHER VARIETY *C. striata* (grows three-times as high, with glossy, leathery leaves; the climbing tendrils stick onto walls).

PLANT PROFILE
HEIGHT 2m (6ft)
SPREAD Indefinite
SITE Bright filtered light
SOIL John Innes No. 2
HARDINESS Min 5°C (41°F)
FLOWERING Summer

Cissus rhombifolia Grape ivy

C

WIDELY GROWN AND VERY POPULAR, a mature, rampant grape ivy is very impressive; the sum of the whole far exceeding the individual parts. The glossy dark green leaves are nearly diamond-shaped and serrated, and the lax stems need to be tied to a group of canes, or to horizontal wires fixed to a wall. Very easy to grow, it can be kept in a pot or border. Water freely in full growth, applying a monthly liquid feed; give just a sparing drink over winter. If growing in a pot, replace the top layer of soil each spring, or move into a larger container. Prune for space in early spring. Susceptible to red spider mites, whiteflies and mealybugs.

PLANT PROFILE
HEIGHT 3m (10ft)
SPREAD Indefinite
SITE Bright filtered light
SOIL John Innes No. 2
HARDINESS Min 5°C (41°F)
FLOWERING Summer

C

x *Citrofortunella microcarpa* Panama orange

THIS NATURAL, CURIOUS CROSS between a citrus and kumquat is an attractive, shrubby evergreen plant with glossy leaves. The waxy flowers usually appear in summer and are followed by small fruit (if being grown indoors, hand-pollinate the flowers using a small brush). The fruit tastes bitter, but it can be used to make marmalade. Prune in late winter or early spring to restrict size, if required. Provide a humid atmosphere indoors. When in full growth, water daily and apply a liquid feed every two to three weeks; at this point, it can also be placed outside. Water sparingly in winter. Red spider mites can be a problem.

PLANT PROFILE
HEIGHT 1m (3ft)
SPREAD 1m (3ft)
SITE Full light filtered from the sun
SOIL John Innes No. 2
HARDINESS Min 10°C (50°F)
FLOWERING Summer

Citrus x *meyeri* 'Meyer' Meyer's Lemon

C

IT IS EASY TO GROW A LEMON TREE that produces masses of fruit. The widely sold Meyer's lemon has glossy, leathery leaves, a nice branching shape and highly scented, star-shaped flowers (*see inset*). It does need a humid winter conservatory (avoid dry living rooms), but can be stood outside in summer; keep it inside until there are constant warm temperatures because it hates sudden changes. The fruit needs 9 to 12 months to ripen. Give the tree a big drink until the water pours out the bottom, then wait until the soil is quite dry before the next watering. Provide a liquid feed from spring to autumn. Beware red spider mites and scale insects.

OTHER VARIETY *C. limon* 'Quatre Saisons' (easier to grow, not needing so much winter humidity – exceptionally prolific).

PLANT PROFILE

HEIGHT	1.8m (6ft)
SPREAD	1.2m (4ft)
SITE	Full light
SOIL	John Innes No. 2
HARDINESS	Min 3–5°C (37–41°F)
FLOWERING	Spring to summer

C | *Clerodendron myricoides* 'Ugandense' Blue glory bower

A BEAUTIFUL EVERGREEN CLIMBER from tropical Africa, the blue glory bower has eye-catching, bright green leaves up to 10cm (4in) long, and curious, blue to violet flowers (sometimes blue and white). With luck, more flowers will appear through winter. Grow it up a series of horizontal wires fixed to a wall or around a pillar, and provide light shade from scorching midday sun. Summer ventilation is equally important. Water freely in full growth and apply a monthly liquid feed; water sparingly over winter. Prune in early spring to restrict its size, and to thin out congested growth. Protect against mealybugs, red spider mites and whiteflies.

OTHER VARIETY *C. x speciosum* (taller and twining, rich green leaves and scarlet flowers).

PLANT PROFILE

HEIGHT 1.8–2.4m (6–8ft)

SPREAD 1.8–2.4m (6–8ft)

SITE Full light

SOIL John Innes No. 3

HARDINESS Min 10°C (50°F)

FLOWERING Summer to autumn

Clianthus puniceus Glory pea

C

THE QUIRKY SHAPE of the bright red flowers on this fun, evergreen, climbing shrub explains why it is also called lobster claw. In the wild, it grows up to 4m (12ft) high, but in a conservatory border with limited root space it will only reach about 2.4m (8ft). If the growth becomes too rampant indoors, cut the plant back in the spring and try it outside against a sunny, sheltered wall in a frost-free site on poor, free-draining soil. Inside or out, prune flowered shoots by up to one-third after flowering. Water freely when in full growth, giving a monthly liquid feed; water sparingly in winter. Add grit to the compost to improve drainage.

OTHER VARIETIES *C. puniceus* 'Albus' (white flowers – *see inset*); *C. puniceus* 'Roseus' (dark rose-pink flowers).

PLANT PROFILE

HEIGHT 2.4m (8ft)

SPREAD 2.4m (8ft)

SITE Full light

SOIL John Innes No. 3 with added grit

HARDINESS Min 3°C (37°F)

FLOWERING Spring to early summer

C

Clivia miniata Kaffir lily

A SOUTH AFRICAN EVERGREEN PERENNIAL, the Kaffir lily makes an extremely attractive houseplant with strap-like leaves (*see inset*). When it is about four years old it will start flowering. The flower spike has around 15 buds on top that slowly separate and open; they range in colour from orange (typically) to yellow and red. Ensure that the compost has good drainage by adding plenty of grit. Water freely when in full growth, providing a weekly liquid feed, but give it a rest in winter with minimal watering. Let the thick roots pack the pot, even to the extent of bulging out of the soil, and only repot the plant every three to four years. Beware mealybugs.

OTHER VARIETIES *C. miniata* 'Aurea' (yellow flowers); *C. miniata* var. *citrina* (creamy-white-yellow flowers).

PLANT PROFILE

HEIGHT 60cm (2ft)

SPREAD 60cm (2ft)

SITE Bright, filtered or indirect light

SOIL John Innes No. 2

HARDINESS Min 10°C (50°F)

FLOWERING Late winter or early spring

Codiaeum 'Flamingo' Croton

C

THESE FLAMBOYANT FOLIAGE PLANTS come from the Pacific Islands and Malaysia. The leaves range from flash yellows to bright reds, and frequently there is more than one colour on the same plant. 'Flamingo' has creamy-veined, young green leaves that turn yellow and end up red or purple. Forget the summer flowers, which rarely appear in a conservatory. Provide shade from the hot sun, avoid draughts and sudden temperature changes that can cause leaf drop, and provide high humidity levels. Water freely while in growth, and apply a liquid feed every two to three weeks; water sparingly with tepid water over winter. Beware scale insects and red spider mites.

OTHER VARIETY *C. variegatum* var. *pictum* (new leaves are green and yellow, older leaves are red).

PLANT PROFILE
HEIGHT 1m (3ft)
SPREAD 1m (3ft)
SITE Full light
SOIL John Innes No. 3
HARDINESS Min 8°C (46°F)
FLOWERING Summer

C

Codiaeum 'Gold Star' Croton

WITH ITS GLOSSY LEATHERY LEAVES that combine green and bright yellow, 'Gold Star' makes a striking focal point and shows up best against a non-white background or the effect is diluted. The summer flowers rarely appear in a conservatory. Provide shade from the hot sun, avoid draughts and sudden temperature changes that can cause leaf drop, and provide high humidity levels. Water freely while in growth, and apply a liquid feed every two to three weeks; water sparingly with tepid water over winter. Protect against scale insects and red spider mites.

OTHER VARIETY *C. variegatum* var. *pictum* 'Evening Embers' (dense and strong growing with bluish-black leaves splashed red and green).

PLANT PROFILE	
HEIGHT 1m (3ft)	
SPREAD 1m (3ft)	
SITE Full light	
SOIL John Innes No. 3	
HARDINESS Min 8°C (46°F)	
FLOWERING Summer	

Columnea x *banksii* Goldfish plant

C

PLACE THIS TROPICAL SOUTH AMERICAN PLANT in a hanging basket where its woody stems will arch up and trail over the sides in thick, tangled growth covered with dark green leaves about 4cm (1½in) long. The leaves contrast nicely with the scarlet, tubular flowers, which have a small hood and a yellow throat. Provide high humidity levels and avoid direct scorching sun. Water freely in full growth using rain- or soft water and apply a one-quarter-strength tomato feed (but only give a sparing drink for the six weeks it is in bud, until the flowers open). Water moderately over winter. Prone to mealybugs and aphids.

OTHER VARIETY *C. gloriosa* (trailing stems with bright red flowers; leaves covered in fine purple hairs).

PLANT PROFILE
HEIGHT To 15cm (6in)
SPREAD To 90cm (3ft)
SITE Bright filtered light
SOIL Loamless potting compost
HARDINESS Min 15°C (59°F)
FLOWERING Spring to autumn

C

Columnea microphylla 'Variegata' Goldfish plant

THE GREY-GREEN LEAVES with narrow cream margins make this columnea an interesting variation on *C. x banksii* (*see p.89*). The woody stems initially grow upwards before arching over the side of a hanging basket and trailing straight down. The tubular, hooded flowers are brash scarlet with a yellow throat. Provide high humidity and keep it out of direct scorching sun. Water freely in full growth using rain- or soft water and apply a one-quarter strength tomato feed (but only water sparingly for the six weeks while in bud, until they open). Avoid overwatering, which is fatal, and water moderately over winter. Susceptible to mealybugs and aphids.

OTHER VARIETY *C.* 'Stavanger' (vigorous and free-branching with dark green leaves and scarlet flowers).

PLANT PROFILE

HEIGHT To 15cm (6in)

SPREAD 1.2m (4ft))

SITE Bright filtered light

SOIL Loamless potting compost

HARDINESS Min 15°C (59°F)

FLOWERING Spring to summer

Cordyline australis 'Variegata' New Zealand cabbage palm

C

THIS TALL-STEMMED TREE – it is not a palm – initially produces one brown trunk topped by a disorderly mop of outward-pointing, strap-like leaves (*see inset*). 'Variegata' has green leaves with creamy-white stripes. When it gets too big for its conservatory pot, it can be grown outside where it should eventually flower, but it must have a sunny, sheltered, frost-free position, as well as a space that exceeds 1.2m (4ft) wide, so that it can be clearly seen. Indoors, water moderately and apply a monthly liquid feed; water sparingly in winter. Replace the top layer of soil every spring or move into a larger pot. Scale insects and red spider mites may be a problem.

OTHER VARIETIES *C. australis* 'Torbay Dazzler' (leaves with bold cream stripes and margins); *C. australis* 'Torbay Red' (red leaves).

PLANT PROFILE	
HEIGHT	1.8m (6ft) or more
SPREAD	1–1.2m (3–4ft)
SITE	Bright filtered light
SOIL	John Innes No. 2
HARDINESS	Half hardy
FLOWERING	Summer

C *Cordyline fruticosa* 'Red Edge' Good luck tree

THE BROAD, GREEN, RED-EDGED LEAVES make the good luck tree a
good choice for the style conscious. Use it as a focal point in a
group of foliage plants, or in a white room to add impact (*see inset*).
In time, the lower mature leaves fall off, leaving a short bare stem
with the most recent foliage on top. It is easy to look after – spray
to create humidity, and keep out of draughts and direct scorching
sun for the best leaf colour. Replace the top layers of soil every
spring or move the plant into a larger pot. Water moderately and
apply a monthly liquid feed; water sparingly in winter. Protect
against scale insects and red spider mites.

OTHER VARIETY *C. fruticosa* 'Lord Robertson' (green and cream
leaves that gradually turn reddish-purple).

PLANT PROFILE
HEIGHT 1m (3ft) or more
SPREAD 60cm (24in)
SITE Bright filtered light
SOIL John Innes No. 2
HARDINESS Min 13°C (55°F)
FLOWERING Summer

Correa backhouseana Australian fuchsia

THE CHUNKY, SHRUBBY AUSTRALIAN FUCHSIA has densely-packed growth with rust-red twigs and dark green leaves. This sets off its long, thin, drooping, tubular flowers, which appear in small clusters and vary in colour, being either pale or reddish-green, or cream. It is best grown in a conservatory border, but can be placed outside in a sunny, sheltered, frost-free site. Grow it in neutral to acid fertile soil that is moist but free-draining. Indoors, ventilate well, and water moderately, adding a monthly liquid feed when in full growth; water sparingly over winter. Beware scale insects.

OTHER VARIETY *C. reflexa* (rich green leaves with bell-shaped, green, white, pink or red flowers).

PLANT PROFILE
HEIGHT 1m (3ft)
SPREAD 1m (3ft)
SITE Full light
SOIL Ericaceous
HARDINESS Half hardy
FLOWERING Late autumn to late spring

C | *Cotyledon orbiculata*

A CURIOUS SOUTH AFRICAN SUCCULENT, *C. orbiculata* has striking leaves that are wavy at the edges, often with a thin red rim. Even better, they have a silvery-frosted coating all over, but must be handled with care or they can easily get marked. The late summer flowers appear on long stems and are red or yellowish-red. Shade from hot sun and water sparingly over summer, then moderately from the end of summer, applying a monthly, diluted nitrogen liquid feed. Keep completely dry over winter. When watering, take care not to splash and mark the leaves. Prone to aphids.

OTHER VARIETY *C. orbiculata* var. *oblonga* (packed, fleshy, wavy-edged, white-coated leaves, and yellowish-red or orange flowers).

PLANT PROFILE

HEIGHT 60cm (24in)

SPREAD 60cm (24in)

SITE Full light

SOIL Cactus compost

HARDINESS Min 7°C (45°F)

FLOWERING Late summer to autumn

Crassula arborescens Silver jade plant

C

THE CHIEF ATTRACTION of this shrub-like succulent lies in its mass of evergreen leaves, which have a grey or even blue tinge and are attached to miniature tree-like stems (*see inset*). Sometimes the leaves also have an attractive red margin and red spots on the top side. In the wild, in South Africa, the pink flowers are star-shaped but they rarely appear in cooler, northern climates. Water moderately from spring to autumn, applying a monthly liquid feed; water sparingly in winter. Mealybugs, vine weevils and aphids may be a problem.

OTHER VARIETY *C. ovata* (twice as tall, resembling a miniature tree with branching stems and small evergreen leaves).

PLANT PROFILE
HEIGHT 90cm (3ft)
SPREAD 90cm (3ft)
SITE Bright filtered light
SOIL Cactus compost
HARDINESS Min 5–7°C (41–45°F)
FLOWERING Late autumn or winter

C

Crassula socialis

SOME CRASSULAS ARE BUSHY and shrub-like in the wild, but the South African *C. socialis* is the creeping dwarf kind; it barely gets above ankle high and will keep on spreading if given enough space. The light green leaves are packed into tight rosettes, with short flower stems reaching up above them, topped by clusters of tiny white flowers. Water moderately from spring to autumn, and apply a monthly liquid feed; water sparingly in winter. Protect against mealybugs, vine weevils and aphids.

OTHER VARIETY *C.* 'Morgan's Beauty' (grows twice as tall – slow spreader with silvery foliage and tiny pink flowers).

PLANT PROFILE
HEIGHT 6cm (2½in)
SPREAD Indefinite
SITE Bright filtered light
SOIL Cactus compost
HARDINESS Min 5–7°C (41–45°F)
FLOWERING Late autumn or winter

Cryptanthus bivittatus Starfish plant

FOR STARTLING COLOURS and strong, starfish shapes, try one of the many tropical, ankle-high, South American cryptanthus plants, also known as earth stars. Each rosette of *C. bivittatus* contains up to about 20 strap-shaped, dark green leaves that stand out for their white or pink stripes. The inconspicuous white flowers appear in midsummer. Provide decent humidity and grow in a shallow container or pot. Water moderately, adding a monthly, diluted liquid feed when in full growth; slightly reduce the watering in winter. Other kinds of starfish plants are available in different colours, some with vivid banding.

OTHER VARIETY *C. zonatus* 'Zebrinus' (the rosette of leaves have vivid green and white bands of colour).

PLANT PROFILE
HEIGHT To 10cm (4in)
SPREAD To 25cm (10in)
SITE Full or bright filtered light
SOIL Bromeliad compost
HARDINESS Min 20°C (68°F)
FLOWERING Summer

C | *Ctenanthe oppenheimiana*

THIS BRIGHTLY PATTERNED FOLIAGE plant from tropical Brazil
has marvellous, paddle-like leathery leaves that can grow up to
40cm (16in) long. They are dark green with broad, V-shaped, silver
markings. Grow it in a pot on a raised shelf if you want to be
able to see the attractive wine-red underside of the leaves. The
insignificant white flowers appear on and off throughout the year.
Provide high humidity levels, a constant temperature and draught-
free conditions. Water freely when in full growth and apply a liquid
feed every three to four weeks; water moderately over winter.
Susceptible to mealybugs.

OTHER VARIETY *C. oppenheimiana* 'Tricolor' (the never-never plant
has creamy-white and pale and dark green markings).

PLANT PROFILE
HEIGHT 1m (3ft)
SPREAD 60cm (24in)
SITE Bright filtered light
SOIL John Innes No. 2
HARDINESS Min 13°C (55°F)
FLOWERING Throughout the year

Cuphea hyssopifolia False heather

C

THE SMALL, BUSHY FALSE HEATHER, native to Mexico, is easily grown in a conservatory border or pot, and can be placed outside in summer. The numerous, small, star-like flowers come in pale purple (*see inset*), pink or white, and are nicely set off against the glossy, dark green leaves that hang on all year. Shade it from hot summer sun and provide some humidity. Water freely when in full growth, giving a liquid feed every three to four weeks; water sparingly in winter. Add grit to the compost to guarantee good drainage, and do not overwater. Beware aphids and whiteflies.

OTHER VARIETY *C. ignea* (*see p. 100*).

PLANT PROFILE

HEIGHT 60cm (24in)

SPREAD 80cm (32in)

SITE Full light

SOIL John Innes No. 2

HARDINESS Min 7°C (45°F)

FLOWERING Summer to autumn

C

Cuphea ignea Cigar flower

THIS STRIKING, BRIGHTLY COLOURED Mexican evergreen is grown for its red tubular flowers, which have one intriguing dark red and one white band at the mouth. Growth is on the bushy side, with glossy, bright green leaves. Shade it from the hot summer sun and provide some humidity. Water freely when in full growth, when it can also be placed outside, and give a balanced liquid feed every three to four weeks. Water sparingly in winter. For good drainage, add grit to the compost. Beware aphids and whiteflies.

OTHER VARIETIES *C. hyssopifolia* (*see p.99*); *C. ignea* 'Variegata' (lime and cream-flecked leaves).

PLANT PROFILE
HEIGHT 30cm (12in)
SPREAD 30cm (12in)
SITE Full light
SOIL John Innes No. 2
HARDINESS Min 7°C (45°F)
FLOWERING Spring to autumn

Cyanotis somaliensis Pussy ears

C

PUSSY EARS MAKES A VERY GOOD CHOICE for a low-growing plant with distinctive foliage – its leathery, olive-green leaves have a gentle covering of white whiskers (hence the common name). The spreading growth also makes it interesting for a conservatory border or hanging basket. The summer flowers are mauve-blue (*see inset*). Water moderately at all times, giving a monthly liquid feed when in full growth, and ensure that any adjacent plants also like fairly dry soil. Avoid overfeeding because it encourages soft, lank growth.

OTHER VARIETY *C. kewensis* (the teddy bear plant is a good spreader with slightly ginger-coloured leaf hairs).

PLANT PROFILE
HEIGHT 15cm (6in)
SPREAD 40cm (16in)
SITE Full light
SOIL John Innes No. 2
HARDINESS Min 10°C (50°F)
FLOWERING Summer

C

Cycas revoluta Japanese sago palm

THE IMPRESSIVE FOLIAGE of the Japanese sago palm has an array of leaves that arches out of the top of the slow-growing trunk, which eventually becomes quite stout (*see inset*). Each leaf is about 90cm (3ft) long and has a central rib with long thin needles arranged on either side; new leaves appear irregularly and infrequently. To ensure all sides get good light, keep turning the plant – also provide average humidity and shade from hot sun. Water moderately when in full growth, but reduce watering and lower the humidity over winter. Plants may suddenly become dormant, then begin inching up again. Protect against red spider mites, mealybugs and scale insects.

OTHER VARIETIES *C. circinalis* (tall robust stem and long, glossy, rich green leaves); *C. media* (also tall and robust, with long leaves).

PLANT PROFILE
HEIGHT 1.7m (5½ft)
SPREAD 1.4m (5ft)
SITE Full light
SOIL Equal parts compost, peat substitute and grit
HARDINESS Min 7–10°C (45–50°F)

Cyclamen persicum 'Sylvia' Florists' cyclamen

C

THIS HIGHLY POPULAR WINTER POT PLANT has two key attractions –
sweet-scented, pinkish-red flowers, and attractive mounds of silver-
patterned, rich green leaves (*see inset*). Provide full winter light and
filtered summer light. Water moderately around the sides when in
full growth, applying a low-nitrogen liquid feed every two weeks.
Reduce watering when the leaves die. Keep the plant dry for
the two to three months it is dormant. When the tuber fills the
container, repot while dormant, keeping the top of the tuber
just above the soil surface. Prone to red spider mites, vine weevils
and mould.

OTHER VARIETY *C.* 'Scentsation' (strongly-scented flowers in pink,
carmine-red or crimson).

PLANT PROFILE	
HEIGHT 23cm (9in)	
SPREAD 23cm (9in)	
SITE Full winter light	
SOIL John Innes No. 2	
HARDINESS Min 10°C (50°F)	
FLOWERING Winter	

C | *Cymbidium* Kings Loch 'Cooksbridge'

YOU DO NOT NEED A SPIDER-PACKED JUNGLE in Borneo to grow orchids, and cymbidium is one of the easiest. 'Cooksbridge' has attractive green flowers with a green and red lip. When planting in a pot, add a bit of charcoal and bone meal to the compost. In summer, provide good ventilation, and ideally stand it outside in a light, shady position with shelter from the wind. If grown indoors, mist the plant every day to create some humidity. Water moderately, giving a liquid orchid feed (available from garden centres and specialist nurseries) every third watering; water sparingly over winter. Beware red spider mites, aphids, whiteflies and mealybugs

OTHER VARIETY *C.* 'Strathbraan' (pale pink winter flowers with attractive red marks around the central part).

PLANT PROFILE

HEIGHT 60cm (24in)

SPREAD 45cm (18in)

SITE Bright filtered light

SOIL Terrestrial orchid compost

HARDINESS Min 10°C (50°F)

FLOWERING Winter

Cyperus involucratus Umbrella grass

C

THIS AFRICAN GRASS grows 12 to 28 outward-pointing, green 'umbrella spokes' at the top of each of its strong stems, with tiny clusters of yellow summer flowers that gradually turn brown. Umbrella grass can be grown in a conservatory pond, but placing it in a border is another option. Provide high humidity levels at all times – often best achieved by standing it in a wide shallow tray of water. If the pot is being placed at the edge of a pond, cover the soil surface with gravel and submerge so that it is 35mm (1⅜in) below the water level. Apply a monthly liquid feed in summer.

OTHER VARIETY *C. alternifolius* (dark green stems and small spikelets of yellow-brown flowers).

PLANT PROFILE
HEIGHT 60–75cm (24–30in)
SPREAD 60–75cm (24–30in)
SITE Bright filtered light
SOIL John Innes No. 2
HARDINESS Min 5–10°C (41–50°F)
FLOWERING Summer

| *Cyphomandra betacea* Tree tomato

THE LARGE, SHRUBBY TREE TOMATO has soft, downy, almost fleshy leaves up to 30cm (12in) long, and is grown for its bright red, supposedly edible fruit, which many people actually find quite disgusting. White to pale pink flowers appear from spring onwards. Though it takes up plenty of space, it can be grown in large pots or a border. Provide decent humidity, and water freely when in full growth, applying a monthly liquid feed; give a sparing drink in winter. Repot or replace the top layers of compost each spring. When the plant is young, nip off the stem tips to induce bushy growth; older plants can be given a light prune after flowering to maintain a balanced shape. Whiteflies and red spider mites may be a problem.

PLANT PROFILE

HEIGHT 2m (6ft) or more

SPREAD 2–3m (6–10ft)

SITE Full or bright filtered light

SOIL John Innes No. 3

HARDINESS Min 5–7°C (41–45°F)

FLOWERING Spring to summer

Cyrtanthus elatus Scarborough lily

C

A FLASHY, BRIGHT RED SOUTH AFRICAN EVERGREEN, Scarborough lily has strap-like leaves that grow up to 45cm (18in) long, and a cluster of open, funnel-shaped, faintly-scented flowers in late summer. It is easily grown on a windowsill. Plant in spring, adding leafmould and sharp sand to the soil, and leave the bulb's neck exposed above the surface. Water freely when in full growth, applying a liquid feed every two to three weeks; water sparingly in winter and keep cool. Thereafter, only repot when the container is packed with roots. It might still be sold as *C. purpureus*, *C. speciosus* or *Vallota speciosa*.

OTHER VARIETY   *C. mackenii* var. *cooperi* (see *p.108*).

PLANT PROFILE
HEIGHT 30–60cm (12–24in)
SPREAD 10cm (4in)
SITE Full light
SOIL John Innes No. 2
HARDINESS Half hardy
FLOWERING Late summer

C **|** *Cyrtanthus mackenii* var. *cooperi* Fire lily

A SOUTH AFRICAN BULB related to the showy amaryllis, the fire lily has four to ten narrow, tubular, faintly-scented yellow or cream flowers (the parent plant, *C. mackenii*, has white flowers). Both kinds can be grown outside, but a sunny, sheltered position is essential, as is a frost-free garden with free-draining soil. In a conservatory, plant the bulbs with their necks flush to the soil, which needs a little extra leafmould and sand. Shade from hot sun and water freely when in full growth, adding a liquid feed every two to three weeks. Water sparingly over winter (in lower temperatures, less water is required). In the garden, plant the bulb at twice its own depth in rich soil.

OTHER VARIETY *C. elatus* (the Scarborough lily has bright scarlet flowers in late summer).

PLANT PROFILE

HEIGHT 20–30cm (8–12in)

SPREAD 10cm (4in)

SITE Bright filtered light

SOIL John Innes No. 2

HARDINESS Half hardy

FLOWERING Spring to summer

Cyrtomium falcatum Japanese holly fern

C

THIS ASIAN EVERGREEN FERN can easily be grown outdoors in a mild, shady, sheltered site, but it may also be grown in a conservatory. The unfolding, glossy, dark green fronds have attractive, holly-like leaves about 5cm (2in) long. Provide humidity on hot summer days and transfer to a larger pot when the roots become congested. Water freely when in growth, when it can also be stood outside, and apply a weak liquid feed every two weeks. Give a moderate drink in winter. It is sometimes still sold and referred to as *Polystichum falcatum*.

OTHER VARIETIES *C. falcatum* 'Rochfordianum' (more deeply cut leaves); *C. fortunei* (pale green fronds).

PLANT PROFILE
HEIGHT 60cm (2ft)
SPREAD 1.1m (3½ft)
SITE Bright indirect light
SOIL 1 part John Innes No. 2 with added bark and charcoal, 2 parts sharp sand, 3 parts leafmould
HARDINESS Half hardy

D

Didymochlaena truncatula

A LUXURIOUS RICH GREEN FERN that comes from Africa, America and Polynesia, *D. truncatula* adds a striking, tropical note to any small pond-side planting in a conservatory, and can also be grown in a grotto with decent light levels. This outward-stretching plant has a good reach without taking up too much space, but note that if you place a group of them too close together, the leaves will smother each other and make it difficult to appreciate their strong architectural shape. These plants are best grown where there is high humidity. Water freely in full growth, giving a monthly liquid feed; keep just moist in winter.

PLANT PROFILE

HEIGHT To 1m (3ft)

SPREAD To 1m (3ft)

SITE Bright filtered light

SOIL 1 part compost, bark and charcoal, 2 parts sharp sand, 3 parts leafmould

HARDINESS Min 10°C (50°F)

Dieffenbachia seguine 'Amoena'   Mother-in-law's tongue   D

THERE ARE SEVERAL VERY GOOD FORMS of *D. seguine*, all of which
have highly attractive leaves. Those of 'Amoena' are green with
creamy-white bands and marbling (*see inset*). Over summer, mist
regularly to provide some humidity, water moderately and apply
a monthly liquid feed. Maintain good light levels over winter and
water sparingly. In spring, move it into a slightly larger pot with
fresh soil. The common name, mother-in-law's tongue, is a jokey
reference to the plant's toxicity, the sap causing a wide range of
effects, from mouth swelling to speech loss, if it is transferred from
fingers to lips; gloves are essential when handling it.

OTHER VARIETIES   *D. seguine* 'Exotica' (creamy-white variegated
leaves); *D. seguine* 'Tropic Snow' (cream feathering on leaves).

PLANT PROFILE	
HEIGHT To 2m (6ft)	
SPREAD 60cm (24in)	
SITE Bright filtered light	
SOIL John Innes No. 3	
HARDINESS Min 15°C (59°F)	
FLOWERING Intermittent	

D | *Dietes bicolor*

A SOUTH AFRICAN BULB, *D.bicolor* produces beautiful, small, deep yellow flowers with a brown mark on the base of its three petals. The pale green, leathery leaves are narrow and sword-like, and tend to stick straight up out of the soil. It is the hardiest dietes available, and can be grown outside in a sunny, sheltered, frost-free site, but the soil should ideally be moist (dry is acceptable) with excellent drainage. In conservatories, water freely when in full growth, but reduce the amount after flowering. Keep the soil just moist when dormant.

OTHER VARIETY *D. iridioides* (the white flowers last one day only, but more keep on coming).

PLANT PROFILE

HEIGHT 60–90cm (24–36in)

SPREAD 30cm (12in)

SITE Full light

SOIL John Innes No. 2

HARDINESS Half hardy

FLOWERING Spring to summer

Dionaea muscipula Venus fly trap

D

THIS IS A GOOD, FUN PLANT that is surprisingly easy to grow. Although new 'traps' keep emerging out of the soil, the more they shut on prey (flies, mosquitoes and small spiders, etc.) the quicker they become exhausted and die. Let the traps feed naturally without extra force-feeding (particularly when children are about). A small pot might easily contain about 15 or more traps in midsummer, when the tiny white flowers appear on a short stalk (*see inset*). Provide full light all year, and stand the pot in a tray filled with pebbles and rainwater. Keep the bottom of the pot submerged in summer (when it also likes fresh air). In winter, the bottom should stay just above the water, but occasionally dip it right in for a drink.

PLANT PROFILE
HEIGHT 10cm (4in)
SPREAD 5cm (2in)
SITE Bright sun
SOIL Carnivorous plant compost
HARDINESS 4°C (39°F)
FLOWERING Summer

D | *Diplarrhena moraea*

SOMETIMES CALLED THE BUTTERFLY IRIS because the flowers resemble those of an iris and look like a swarm of butterflies. The white flowers, with yellow and purple markings on the inner petals, are perched on long thin stems, and the often sword-like, evergreen leaves are about 45cm (18in) long. Coming from the hotter climates of Tasmania and south-east Australia, *D. moraena* must either be grown outside in a warm part of the garden, or in a conservatory border where it should not fail. Outside, provide moist but free-draining, sandy, rich soil, possibly in partial shade. Inside, add sand to the compost to make it free draining. Water well in full growth, and rather less over winter.

PLANT PROFILE

HEIGHT 60cm (24in)

SPREAD 23cm (9in)

SITE Bright filtered light

SOIL Loamless potting compost

HARDINESS Frost hardy

FLOWERING Late spring and early summer

Dracaena marginata 'Tricolor' Madagascar dragon tree

DRACAENAS MAKE VERY GOOD FEATURE foliage plants. *D. marginata* has a slender vertical trunk (which eventually starts branching), topped by an array of long, thin evergreen leaves, while the popular 'Tricolor' has creamy stripes with a hint of red at the leaf edges. Although it can get quite tall, it is very slow growing and may take several years to flower. Provide average humidity and shade from hot sun. Water freely from spring to autumn, applying a monthly liquid feed; water sparingly over winter. Each spring replace the top layers of soil or move into a slightly larger pot if necessary. Red spider mites may be a problem.

OTHER VARIETIES *D. fragrans* Deremensis Group (with various leaf colours – *see inset*); *D. marginata* 'Colorama' (red-edged leaves).

PLANT PROFILE

HEIGHT 1.8m (6ft) or more

SPREAD 1m (3ft) or more

SITE Full light

SOIL John Innes No. 3

HARDINESS Min 13°C (55°F)

FLOWERING Summer

D | *Drosera capensis* Cape sundew

A NIFTY LITTLE CARNIVOROUS PLANT, cape sundew has a congested mass of long, thin, tentacle-like leaves with reddish hairs at the end, which are tipped with a sticky, glistening substance (hence the common name). Insects landing on it quickly become ensnared. This sends a message to other tentacles, which creep towards the victim, smearing it with more 'glue' and eventually forcing it down, where it is digested and absorbed in fluids. A fun way to get rid of mosquitoes. Shade from hot sun, and keep the compost continually moist by standing the pot in a saucer of rain- or soft water. Visit a nursery specializing in carnivorous plants to see a wide range.

OTHER VARIETIES *D. gigantea* (erect and vigorous with white flowers); *D. rotundifolia* (hardy; grow it outside in a bog garden).

PLANT PROFILE
HEIGHT To 30cm (12in)
SPREAD To 15cm (6in)
SITE Full light
SOIL Carnivorous plant compost
HARDINESS Min 2°C (36°F)
FLOWERING Spring to autumn

Duchesnea indica Indian strawberry

D

THE LOW-GROWING INDIAN STRAWBERRY, also known as mock strawberry, produces small flowers followed by bright red fruit, but it does not taste anything like traditional strawberries; in fact the fruit is quite inedible. Still, it is an attractive, easy-to-grow plant, with evergreen rosettes of fleshy, silver-grey leaves. In the wild, it thrives in shaded, woodland sites in India, China and Indonesia and needs to be kept well away from direct sun in a conservatory. It can be placed outside over summer, but if the plant is being kept inside, provide good ventilation.

OTHER VARIETY *D. indica* 'Harlequin' (red-tinged foliage speckled with white).

PLANT PROFILE
HEIGHT 10cm (4in)
SPREAD To 1.2m (4ft)
SITE Filtered light
SOIL John Innes No. 2
HARDINESS -15°C (5°F)
FLOWERING Early and late summer

D *Dudleya pulverulenta*

THE SUCCULENT DUDLEYAS often have an attractive silvery covering on the leaves, and this particular species certainly has it, giving year-round interest. It sits firmly on the soil with a rosette of leaves pointing upwards. In spring or early summer, it sends up an astonishingly tall stem, up to 1.5m (5ft) high, but more usually 80cm (32in), with red to yellow star-shaped flowers. Keep in a dry atmosphere, with moderate watering in growth, and a monthly feed. Water sparingly over summer when it is semi-dormant. Protect against mealybugs.

OTHER VARIETY *D. brittonii* (the silver dollar plant has leaves with a striking white covering, and pale yellow flowers).

PLANT PROFILE
HEIGHT <u>20cm (8in)</u>
SPREAD 60cm (24in)
SITE Full light
SOIL Cactus compost
HARDINESS Min 7°C (45°F)
FLOWERING Spring or early summer

Echeveria pulvinata Plush plant

E

THE EVERGREEN ECHEVERIAS make extremely attractive, highly distinctive plants, many of which are excellent for planting outside over summer at the front edge of a border, creating various patterns. The bushy plant has felt-like brown stems, each producing a rosette of small, fleshy leaves covered in fine white hairs; in autumn, the leaf margins turn red. From late winter to early spring, the stems produce small, flashy yellow or red-yellow flowers. Water moderately while in growth, applying a half-strength liquid feed each month. Keep just moist over winter. Excellent drainage is vital when grown outside and in pots.

OTHER VARIETY *E. derenbergii* (spreads by half the amount; yellow flowers).

PLANT PROFILE
HEIGHT 30cm (12in)
SPREAD 50cm (20in)
SITE Full light
SOIL Standard cactus compost
HARDINESS Min 7°C (45°F)
FLOWERING Winter to early summer

E

Elatostema repens var. repens

A CREEPING, EVERGREEN ASIAN PERENNIAL, *E. repens* is grown for its attractive rounded leaves, which are muted blackish-green above with irregular markings that are either grey or pale green and sometimes develop a bronze flush. The undersides of the leaves are tinged pink, with purple margins. The flowers are completely insignificant. Place it in a border as underplanting for taller, more dramatic plants. Water freely when in full growth, and apply a monthly liquid feed; give a moderate drink over winter.

OTHER VARIETY *E. repens* var. *pulchrum* (initially hairy stem with a purple tint; oblong leaves).

PLANT PROFILE
HEIGHT 10cm (4in)
SPREAD To 60cm (24in)
SITE Bright indirect light
SOIL Loamless potting compost
HARDINESS Min 13°C (55°F)
FLOWERING Summer

Ensete ventricosum Abyssinian banana

E

A BANANA TREE NEEDS PLENTY OF SPACE, whether grown inside or out. Plant it in the garden over summer in a sheltered hot spot where its huge, paddle-shaped, olive-green leaves add plenty of zip to a jungly border, but bring it inside over winter. Its maximum height in a 75cm (2½ft) pot will be about 3.6m (12ft). It will only take three to four years to reach this height but you can stop it getting too tall by using a breadknife to saw off the top 45cm (18in), or more, in midsummer; it will then produce new leaves lower down. In full growth, give it copious drinks of water, applying a monthly liquid feed; water sparingly over winter.

OTHER VARIETY *E. ventricosum* 'Maurelii' (deep red tinge on top of the leaf).

PLANT PROFILE
HEIGHT 3.6m (12ft)
SPREAD 1.8m (6ft)
SITE Full light
SOIL John Innes No. 3
HARDINESS Min 7°C (45°F)
FLOWERING Summer

E

Epipremnum aureum 'Marble Queen' Devil's ivy

A REMARKABLE CLIMBER, devil's ivy is related to a wild species that grows in the Solomon Islands. It has predominantly white leaves with an eye-catching scattering of yellow, cream and green. 'Marble Queen' can be grown up moss poles or as a trailer with the stems dangling down. It is not fussy and will tolerate less than ideal conditions, but give it a light prune in early spring to make it branch out and keep it from spreading too far. Water freely over summer, adding a monthly liquid feed; water moderately in winter. Beware scale insects and red spider mites.

OTHER VARIETY *E. aureum* (the parent plant, with large, hand-size leaves, can hit a magnificent 12m/40ft given warm, humid conditions).

PLANT PROFILE
HEIGHT To 2.4m (8ft)
SPREAD Indefinite
SITE Full light
SOIL John Innes No. 3
HARDINESS Min 16–21°C (61–70°F)

Episcia cupreata Carpet plant

E

A SMALL-LEAVED SOUTH AMERICAN PLANT, the carpet plant is what gardening books tend to describe as mat-forming because it spreads rampantly along the ground. Use it in the conservatory border to cover the soil with deep copper-green leaves and provide some colour beneath taller feature plants. Occasionally, the red and yellow flowers will have purple spots in the throat. Add some vermiculite to the soil to open it up and facilitate drainage. Also provide high humidity and water freely over summer, applying a one-quarter strength feed to each watering.

OTHER VARIETY *E.* 'Pink Panther' (leaves have a silvery-green centre, with red flowers).

PLANT PROFILE
HEIGHT 15cm (6in)
SPREAD Indefinite
SITE Bright filtered light
SOIL Loamless compost
HARDINESS Min 15°C (59°F)
FLOWERING Spring to autumn

E

Episcia dianthiflora Carpet plant

SOMETIMES CALLED THE MEXICAN LACE FLOWER, this episcia makes a beautiful plant for a hanging basket. The growth comes dangling out of the container, with dark green leaves that are initially roundish, often with purple-red veins. The flowers are the highlight and have five, frilly-edged white 'petals' flaring out around the opening of each tube (*see inset*). Add some vermiculite to the soil to open it up and facilitate drainage. Also provide high humidity and water freely over summer, applying a one-quarter strength feed to each watering; keep just moist in winter.

OTHER VARIETY *E.* 'Cygnet' (purple-spotted white leaves and light green leaves).

PLANT PROFILE
HEIGHT 15cm (6in)
SPREAD 30cm (12in)
SITE Bright filtered light
SOIL Loamless compost
HARDINESS Min 13°C (55°F)
FLOWERING Spring to summer

Euphorbia milii var. *tulearensis* Crown of thorns

E

PLANT PROFILE

THE TWO BIG ATTRACTIONS of this slow-growing, bushy Madagascan plant are the clusters of pink flowers set against the bright green leaves. Note that the stems have extremely nasty thorns, and need careful handling. Crown of thorns should be grown over winter in a conservatory pot, but it can be placed in a sheltered hot spot outdoors for the summer (*see inset*). Water moderately when in full growth and over the summer, but give a much more sparing drink in winter. Note that all parts are toxic, and that the sap may irritate the skin. Prune when flowering is over – cutting back the stems to a bud – and wear protective gloves.

HEIGHT 1m (3ft)

SPREAD 1m (3ft)

SITE Bright sun

SOIL Free-draining and light

HARDINESS Min 12°C (54°F)

FLOWERING Spring or summer

OTHER VARIETY *E. milii* (bright red flowers with a dash of yellow).

E | *Euphorbia pulcherrima* 'Lilo White' **Poinsettia**

BRIGHT RED POINSETTIAS sell by the zillion at Christmas, but this white form makes a nice contrast. The trick is getting one to produce the same colourful bracts next year. First, cut back the stems in spring once the leaves have fallen, leaving 10cm (4in) high lengths. Leave virtually dry until early summer and then repot and start watering, forcing up new shoots – remove all but the four or so strongest. In early autumn, follow a rigid routine – keep the plant in darkness for 14 hours (cover it up with black polythene in early evening) every day for two months. Water and give a weak liquid feed every two weeks. If it fails... buy a new one.

OTHER VARIETIES   *E. pulcherrima* (traditional, bright red bracts); *E. pulcherrima* 'Ecke's White' (white bracts).

PLANT PROFILE
HEIGHT 22cm (9in)
SPREAD 35cm (14in)
SITE Full light
SOIL 3 parts John Innes No. 2 to 1 part grit, with added bark and leafmould
HARDINESS Min 13–15°C (55–59°F)
FLOWERING Winter

Exacum affine Persian violet

E

A DELIGHTFULLY PRETTY ANNUAL, the Persian violet has a cluster of shiny leaves and a profusion of yellow-centred, lavender-blue, rose-pink or white flowers in summer. Buy a ready-planted pot or sow the seed in early spring. Fill a pot with multi-purpose compost that has had one-third sharp sand mixed in, and moisten with warm water. Scatter the seed on the compost surface and then barely cover with a drizzle of fine compost. Stand out of direct sun at 18°C (64°F). When a few leaves have opened, transfer the plant to a pot of multi-purpose compost (without added sand). Water freely in summer and apply a liquid feed every two to three weeks.

OTHER VARIETIES *E. affine* 'Blue Gem' (compact with lavender-blue flowers); *E. affine* 'White Midget' (pure white flowers).

PLANT PROFILE
HEIGHT 30cm (12in)
SPREAD 30cm (12in)
SITE Full light
SOIL John Innes No. 2
HARDINESS Min 7–10°C (45–50°F)
FLOWERING Summer

F

Fascicularia pitcairniifolia

THIS DISTINCTIVE, CHILEAN FOLIAGE PLANT has a rosette of long, thin evergreen leaves that are green with touches of greyish-white, edged with short brown spines. The best reason for buying it is because the inner portion of its rosette turns flashy red as the tiny blue or bright violet flowers appear. Good ventilation is important and, when in full growth, water moderately and apply a monthly nitrogen feed; water sparingly in winter. If it is being planted outdoors over summer, make sure that it has poor soil with excellent drainage. Beware greenfly while in flower in summer.

OTHER VARIETY *F. bicolor* (the inner portion of the tightly-packed leaves are bright crimson when in flower).

PLANT PROFILE

HEIGHT 1m (3ft)

SPREAD 1m (3ft)

SITE Full light

SOIL Terrestrial bromeliad compost

HARDINESS Min 7°C (45°F)

FLOWERING Summer

Fatsia japonica Japanese fatsia

F

A SUPERB EVERGREEN with big, bold, shiny leaves, the Japanese fatsia has creamy-white flowers in the autumn followed by black berries. It can be grown indoors or out. If kept indoors all year, it must have good ventilation, especially over summer to avoid sudden rises in temperature. If placed outside, the plant will need a sunny or lightly-shaded, sheltered corner because it is not completely hardy – if planted in a summer border, it should have moist, but free-draining soil. Should it get too lanky, then cut back the stems, ideally in spring. Water moderately when in full growth and apply a monthly liquid feed; give a sparing drink in winter.

OTHER VARIETIES *F. japonica* 'Moseri' (more compact, with slightly larger leaves); *F. japonica* 'Variegata' (cream-tipped leaves – *see inset*).

PLANT PROFILE

HEIGHT To 1.8m (6ft)

SPREAD To 1.8m (6ft)

SITE Bright filtered light

SOIL John Innes No. 3

HARDINESS Frost hardy

FLOWERING Autumn

F *Faucaria tigrina* Tiger jaws

THE LOW-GROWING SUCCULENT, tiger jaws, has greyish-green leaves and comes from South Africa, where it grows in rocky, semi-desert areas. The spiny edges of its fleshy, diamond-shaped leaves make them appear like miniature gaping jaws (hence the common name), but the spines are actually very soft and not dangerous (*see inset*). Its best time of year is in autumn, when dozens of golden-yellow, frilly-petalled flowers open, sometimes from red buds. Tiger jaws can be placed or planted outside over summer in extremely free-draining soil. Water moderately when in full growth and apply a low-nitrogen monthly feed; water sparingly in winter.

OTHER VARIETY *F. felina* (clump-forming, spreading succulent with white-spotted leaves and golden-yellow autumn flowers).

PLANT PROFILE

HEIGHT 10cm (4in)

SPREAD 20cm (8in)

SITE Full light

SOIL Standard cactus compost

HARDINESS Min 7°C (45°F)

FLOWERING Autumn

Ferocactus latispinus Barrel cactus

F

THE BARREL CACTUS MAY BE ATTRACTIVE, but it is also incredibly vicious with its ferocious spines (its other names include crow's claw and devil's tongue). Pronounced greyish-green ribs run the length of its rounded shape, and it has 6–15 yellow spines that tend to stick out – the four central ones are red, the lowest ones flattened and hooked. It is a surprise to see this tough, arid-looking cactus flower so colourfully in the summer when it bears bell-shaped, white, red, purple or yellow flowers. Water freely in full growth, and apply a monthly liquid feed; keep dry in winter (mist on warm days). Protect against mealybugs.

OTHER VARIETY *F. cylindraceus* (long, often hooked spines, warty ribs, and orange or yellow flowers).

PLANT PROFILE

HEIGHT 25cm (10in)

SPREAD 40cm (16in)

SITE Full light

SOIL Standard cactus compost

HARDINESS Min 7°C (45°F)

FLOWERING Summer

Ficus benjamina 'Variegata' Weeping fig

THE GENES OF THE WEEPING FIG send it up to 30m (100ft) or so in Southeast Asia, but in a pot you can easily limit this to about head high. Though a cliché in most offices, it is a superb evergreen plant when grown well and set against a strong, upright cane to show off its slender, arching, weeping stems and small, thin, dark green leaves with white edges. The leaves quickly become dusty and need an occasional wipe to keep them looking healthy and shiny. Water moderately in full growth and apply a monthly high-nitrogen feed; keep moist in winter. Prone to red spider mites, mealybugs and scale insects.

OTHER VARIETY *F. longifolia* (glossy leaves and a vertical, tree-like shape).

PLANT PROFILE
HEIGHT 1.8m (5¾ft)
SPREAD 1.2m (4ft)
SITE Full or filtered light
SOIL John Innes No. 3
HARDINESS Min 15°C (59°F)

Ficus bennendijkii 'Alii' Fig

AN EXCELLENT ALTERNATIVE to the kind of figs found standing to
attention in offices and entrance halls, 'Alii' has thin stems and the
kind of shaggy outpouring of long, narrow leaves that makes it an
excellent feature or background plant (*see inset*). Being quite thin, it
is also easy to fit into a relatively tight space, but it must get decent
light. Water moderately when in full growth and apply a monthly
high-nitrogen feed; keep moist in winter. Red spider mites,
mealybugs and scale insects may be a problem.

PLANT PROFILE

HEIGHT 2m (6ft) or more

SPREAD 75cm (30in)

SITE Bright filtered light

SOIL John Innes No. 3

HARDINESS Min 16–21°C
(61–70°F)

| F | *Ficus deltoidea* Mistletoe fig |

THE SLOW-GROWING, SHRUBBY MISTLETOE FIG, found growing
from south-east Asia to Borneo, is relatively small for a ficus and
is chiefly grown for its scattering of sporadic, tiny fruit. The round,
inedible figs appear in pairs, and start off dull yellow before turning
much brighter orange and red. They are set off by the leathery,
spoon-shaped, bright green leaves. Its modest growth makes it
a good choice if there is no room for the spreading, tree-like figs.
Water moderately when in full growth and apply a monthly high-
nitrogen feed; keep moist in winter. Susceptible to red spider mites,
mealybugs and scale insects.

OTHER VARIETY *F. deltoidea* var. *diversifolia* (with rounded or
notched leaves).

PLANT PROFILE

HEIGHT 2m (6ft)

SPREAD 45cm (18in)

SITE Bright filtered light

SOIL John Innes No. 3

HARDINESS Min 16 21°C
(61–70°F)

Ficus elastica 'Doescheri' Indian rubber fig

F

A GIANT TREE reaching 60m (200ft) high in the wilds of tropical India and Java, the Indian rubber fig can be kept much smaller in a conservatory pot. Unlike the arching *F. benjamina*, 'Doescheri' is virtually straight stemmed, and has large, leathery, grey-green, creamy-yellow leaves and pink stalks. The leaves quickly become dusty and need an occasional wipe to stay looking healthy and shiny. Water moderately in full growth and apply a monthly high-nitrogen feed; keep moist in winter. Beware red spider mites, mealybugs and scale insects.

OTHER VARIETIES *F. elastica* (dark green leaves); *F. elastica* 'Decora' (oval leaves with a red flush on the bottom side); Inset: *F. elastica* 'Robusta' (glossy, leathery leaves).

PLANT PROFILE
HEIGHT 2.4m (8ft)
SPREAD 1.2m (4ft)
SITE Full or filtered light
SOIL John Innes No. 3
HARDINESS Min 15°C (59°F)

F

Ficus lyrata Banjo fig

DESPITE BEING A HUGE TREE from tropical west and central Africa, the banjo fig can be grown as a relatively small conservatory plant (*see inset*). It has fiddle-shaped, dark green leaves, much bigger in its native habitat, but in other respects is quite similar to the Indian rubber fig, *F. elastica* (*see p.135*). The banjo fig's leaves can get covered in thick layers of dust and need an occasional wipe to keep them looking healthy and shiny. Water moderately in full growth and apply a monthly high-nitrogen feed; keep moist in winter. Protect against red spider mites, mealybugs and scale insects.

OTHER VARIETIES *F. benjamina* (more graceful, arching growth); *F. elastica* (dark green leaves).

PLANT PROFILE

HEIGHT 1.2–1.8m (4–6ft)

SPREAD 1.2m (4ft)

SITE Full or filtered light

SOIL John Innes No. 3

HARDINESS Min 15°C (59°F)

Ficus pumila Climbing fig, Creeping fig

F

AN EVERGREEN, CREEPING, CLIMBING plant from the Far East, it is tailor-made for a hanging basket, or for a pot that has been securely nailed to a wall. The stems trail over the sides, dangling down with their thin, glossy, heart-shaped leaves. The creeping fig can also be used to cover the soil in a conservatory border that is looking particularly bare, or try growing it up a moss stick. Prune back excess, straggly growth at any time of the year. Mist to provide some humidity if in a hot, dry atmosphere. Water moderately when in full growth, and apply a monthly high-nitrogen feed; keep moist in winter. Prone to red spider mites, mealybugs and scale insects.

OTHER VARIETY *F. pumila* 'Minima' (about half as tall).

PLANT PROFILE

HEIGHT 10cm (4in)	
SPREAD 60cm (2ft)	
SITE Full or filtered light	
SOIL John Innes No. 3	
HARDINESS Min 5–7°C (41–45°F)	

F

Fittonia verschaffeltii 'Janita'   Painted net leaf

RELATED TO TROPICAL PERUVIAN RAINFOREST PLANTS, painted net leaf spreads across the soil when given light shade and high humidity. The leaves are the big attraction with their ornamental network of bright pink veins set against an olive green background. It can be grown in a conservatory border or pot, but the need for constant high humidity levels means it is more easily grown in a terrarium (a large container or bottle made of plastic or glass). Water moderately, keeping the compost just moist (but avoid overwatering at all costs, because the stems will rot). Apply a monthly liquid feed when in full growth.

OTHER VARIETY   *F. verschaffeltii* var. *argyroneura* (silvery-white veins on leaves).

PLANT PROFILE

HEIGHT 15cm (6in)

SPREAD 30cm (12in) or more

SITE Indirect light

SOIL Loamless potting compost

HARDINESS Min 15°C (59°F)

Freesia 'Everatt'

F

BEAUTIFUL, SWEETLY-SCENTED FREESIAS come in a wide range of colours, from soft pastels and yellows to flashy reds like 'Everatt'. They can be either bought ready-potted in winter or grown from small bulbs. Plant bulbs in batches, from the end of summer into autumn, in pots to flower from late winter to spring. Set them 6cm (2½in) apart, with the tops just below the soil surface. Insert small vertical twigs around the outside of the pot (tying string around them) to provide support. Water moderately, increasing the frequency as growth shoots up. When the flower buds appear, give a liquid feed every two weeks.

OTHER VARIETIES *F.* 'Elan' (lilac-purple flowers); *F.* 'Oberon' (yellow flowers, red inside); inset: *F.* 'Blue heaven'.

PLANT PROFILE

HEIGHT To 40cm (16in)

SITE Full light

SOIL John Innes No. 2

HARDINESS Half hardy

FLOWERING Late winter and early spring

F *Fuchsia arborescens* Lilac fuchsia

MORE LIKE A SMALL EVERGREEN TREE than a pot plant, the lilac fuchsia comes from Mexico and central America. Its growth is impressively erect, and the clusters of small summer flowers appear in one flush. The blooms have rose to magenta or purple-pink tubes leading to rose-purple 'wings', with a pale mauve section beneath. Although it can be grown in a pot, it prefers a conservatory border where its roots are not cramped. Ventilate well in summer and ensure it has moderate humidity all year, especially in winter when it hates a hot, dry atmosphere. Water freely in full growth, adding a monthly liquid feed; keep just moist in winter.

OTHER VARIETY *F. fulgens* (pale red and red flowers; 1.5m/5ft high, needs a minimum of 5°C/41°F).

PLANT PROFILE	
HEIGHT To 2m (6ft)	
SPREAD To 1.7m (5½ft)	
SITE Bright filtered light	
SOIL John Innes No. 3	
HARDINESS Half hardy	
FLOWERING Summer	

Fuchsia 'Swingtime'

F

IDEAL FOR A BORDER, POT OR HANGING BASKET, 'Swingtime' has a scarlet tube just above the main flower, which has brash, bright red 'wings' and a white, fluffy, full-bodied 'skirt'. Growth is upright but on the lax side, which means it can be grown in a hanging basket if the branches are allowed to grow out unpruned and small weights are tied to the ends to pull them down. If in a pot, it can be placed outside over summer (avoid full sun). Moderate humidity is important, especially over winter, to avoid a hot, dry atmosphere. Water freely in full growth, adding a monthly liquid feed; keep just moist in winter. Prune hard in early spring and repot.

OTHER VARIETIES *F.* 'Bicentennial' (orange, red flowers); *F.* 'La Campanella' (white, purple flowers); *F.* 'Tom West' (red, purple flowers).

PLANT PROFILE
HEIGHT 30–60cm (12–24in)
SPREAD 45–75cm (18–30in)
SITE Bright filtered light
SOIL John Innes No. 3
HARDINESS Half hardy
FLOWERING Summer

G | *Gardenia augusta* 'Veitchii'

ONE OF THE MOST SENSATIONALLY SCENTED PLANTS, 'Veitchii' has small, green, shiny leaves and beautiful, pure white, double flowers. If grown in a pot it stays quite small, but in a conservatory border it can reach 1.2m (4ft) high. Gardenias can certainly be quite tricky to grow unless they are kept at a constant, warmish temperature – at least 16°C (61°F) when the buds are developing – and out of draughts. Provide average humidity, and only give a drink with rain- or soft water, with an added liquid feed every four weeks in the summer; water sparingly over winter. Beware whiteflies and mealybugs. Well worth trying.

OTHER VARIETIES *G. augusta* (single flowers, slightly smaller leaves and not quite so upright). *G. augusta* 'Mystery' (very compact).

PLANT PROFILE
HEIGHT 1.2m (4ft)
SPREAD 1.2m (4ft)
SITE Bright filtered light
SOIL Ericaceous
HARDINESS Min 10°C (50°F)
FLOWERING Summer to autumn

Gerbera jamesonii Barberton daisy

G

THIS POPULAR, FUN PERENNIAL from South Africa makes an excellent pot plant with its long show of flowers from spring to summer. The daisy like flowers are bright orange-scarlet with a yellow eye, and appear on long, thin stalks above the large, green, thickish leaves, which have a hairy covering on the underside. It can be placed outside over summer (when it likes good ventilation), or planted at the front of a border, but dig it up in early autumn and keep inside over winter. Water freely from spring on and apply a liquid feed every four weeks; keep moist in winter. Repot each spring or replace the top layer of soil

OTHER VARIETY   *G. jamesonii* 'Californian Giants' (flowers in shades of yellow, apricot, orange, red, and pink).

PLANT PROFILE
HEIGHT 30–45cm
SPREAD 30–45cm
SITE Bright filtered light
SOIL John Innes No. 2
HARDINESS Min 5°C (41°F)
FLOWERING Late spring to late summer

G | *Glechoma hederacea* 'Variegata' Variegated ground ivy

A VERY GOOD CHOICE if you need a non-showy plant to cover the border soil with evergreen leaves. Its prodigious growth means that only a few plants are required to provide this leafy base beneath more dominant feature plants. The rounded to kidney-shaped leaves are quite attractive, and have a soft pale green colour with pure white marbling, especially around the margins. From midsummer on, the plants produce tiny, tubular, lilac-mauve flowers similar to those of a nettle. Add some horticultural sand or grit to the soil to make it more free-draining, and water well over summer, but less frequently in winter. Beware slugs and snails.

OTHER VARIETY *G. hederacea* (more vigorous, no marbling on the leaves).

PLANT PROFILE
HEIGHT To 15cm (6in)
SPREAD To 2m (6ft) or more
SITE Full sun or partial shade
SOIL John Innes No. 2
HARDINESS Fully hardy
FLOWERING Summer

Gloriosa superba Glory lily

A TROPICAL, SOUTH AFRICAN, DECIDUOUS CLIMBER, this stupendous plant has large flowers consisting of six red or purple petals, sometimes with a yellow margin, which stand out against its bright green leaves. Because the stems are quite flimsy and weak, the tendrils must have something to grab on to, ideally a series of horizontal wires against a wall or a number of canes with wire wrapped around them. Plants are often sold as tubers (a form of bulb) in early spring; plant upright, 8cm (3½in) deep, adding grit to the compost, and keep at 16°C (60°F). Initially water gently, then freely, applying a liquid feed every two weeks; keep dry over winter.

OTHER VARIETY *G. superba* 'Rothschildiana' (a popular form with bright red flowers, yellow at the base).

PLANT PROFILE

HEIGHT To 2m (6ft)

SPREAD 30cm (12in)

SITE Full light

SOIL John Innes No. 2

HARDINESS Min 8–10°C (46–50°F

FLOWERING Summer to autumn

G

Graptopetalum bellum

THIS SUPERB, LITTLE MEXICAN SUCCULENT has tightly-packed rosettes of fleshy, grey (possibly blue or greenish), pointed leaves that slightly resemble those of an echeveria (*see page 119*). Eventually it will form a small clump and produce a terrific show of pretty, star-shaped, long-lasting, pink to deep red flowers on thin stems. It is easily grown, but needs free-draining soil with added grit to open up the compost. Water freely in spring and summer, adding a low-nitrogen liquid feed every six to eight weeks. Keep barely moist in autumn and winter because leaving it in cold wet soil can be fatal.

OTHER VARIETY *G. paraguayense* (slightly taller with a wide spread; also grey-green leaves and red-spotted white flowers).

PLANT PROFILE
HEIGHT 5–7cm (2–3in)
SPREAD To 15cm (6in)
SITE Full light or bright filtered light
SOIL John Innes No. 2
HARDINESS Min 5°C (41°F)
FLOWERING Late spring to summer

Graptopetalum paraguayense Mother of pearl plant

G

MOTHER OF PEARL PLANTS have rosettes of pointy leaves that are initially pale mauve-grey before turning pinkish–grey–green – they look best when they have mounded up into clumps. The flowers appear on short, thin stems and open from late winter, before those of the similar and popular (but less prodigious) *G. bellum*. Mother of pearl also has slightly more striking white flowers with red spots. It needs free-draining soil with added grit to open up the compost. Water freely in spring and summer, adding a half-strength nitrogen liquid feed every six to eight weeks. Keep barely moist in autumn and winter because it hates sitting in cold wet soil.

OTHER VARIETY *G. bellum* (grey leaves with star-shaped, long-lasting, pink to deep red flowers).

PLANT PROFILE
HEIGHT To 20cm (8in)
SPREAD Indefinite
SITE Full light or bright filtered light
SOIL John Innes No. 2
HARDINESS Min 5°C (41°F)
FLOWERING Late winter and early spring

G | *Grevillea robusta* Silky oak

A GOOD EXAMPLE OF A FAST-GROWING Australian tree that can also be grown as a tall pot plant (*see inset*). The big attraction lies in the graceful, see-through, fern-like leaves on young plants, but note that from about three years old they become much less lacily attractive. Either let it grow taller or replace with a more attractive, young plant. Over summer, try planting it outdoors at the front of a bedding scheme. Indoors, occasionally mist to provide it with some humidity, and repot when the roots start poking out of the drainage holes. Water freely when in full growth, but sparingly in winter, when it also needs good ventilation on sunny days.

OTHER VARIETY *G. banksii* (tall at 2.4m/8ft high, with red, pink or white flowers intermittently throughout the year).

PLANT PROFILE

HEIGHT 2m (6ft)

SPREAD 75cm (30in)

SITE Full light

SOIL Lime-free (ericaceous)

HARDINESS Min 5°C (41°F)

Guzmania monostachia

IN PARTS OF AMERICA AND THE WEST INDIES, G. monostachia grows on a host tree, but it can be easily grown without support in a pot, which is an excellent way to show off its striking flowers and foliage. The pale green or yellowish-green leaves can reach an impressive 40cm (16in) long, and the tubular, white flowers emerge out of dramatic bright red or white parts. Once the flowers die, the leaves also fade away, and a new young plant – attached to the parent – takes over. Provide humidity by misting it with soft water in the early morning, and give only moderate drinks; occasionally pour rainwater into the central cup of leaves. Prone to mealybugs.

OTHER VARIETY G. lingulata var. minor (showy, bright red flower-like growths).

PLANT PROFILE

HEIGHT To 40cm (16in)	
SPREAD To 40cm (16in)	
SITE Bright filtered or indirect light	
SOIL Epiphytic bromeliad compost	
HARDINESS Min 15°C (59°F)	
FLOWERING Summer	

G | *Gynura aurantiaca* Purple velvet plant

THIS EASILY-GROWN INDONESIAN FOLIAGE PLANT has deep-green serrated leaves about 15cm (6in) long, with a soft covering of purple hairs. The orange-yellow flowers appear mainly in winter, but the buds are often snipped off because the flowers reek, you avoid a hideous colour clash with the purple hairs, and you get more leaves. Although growth is initially upright, it eventually becomes much more trailing. Water freely over summer, adding a monthly liquid feed; give a sparing drink in winter (when it also needs bright light) to stop the soil from completely drying out. Susceptible to aphids and red spider mites.

OTHER VARIETY *G. aurantiaca* 'Purple Passion' (more trailing and vigorous growth, with purple-haired stems and leaves).

PLANT PROFILE
HEIGHT To 30cm (12in)
SPREAD 40cm (16in)
SITE Bright filtered light
SOIL John Innes No. 2
HARDINESS Min 13°C (55°F)
FLOWERING Winter

Hardenbergia violacea f. *alba* 'White Crystal' Purple coral pea

H

PLANT PROFILE

HEIGHT 2m (6ft) or more

SITE Full light

SOIL John Innes No. 2

HARDINESS Half hardy

FLOWERING Late winter

AN EVERGREEN TWINING CLIMBER, whose parent grows wild in southern Australia, purple coral pea produces attractive clusters of pea-like flowers at the end of winter. Provide canes or horizontal wall wires to support the vigorous woody growth, shade it from the hot sun and give low to average humidity. Water moderately in the growing season, applying a monthly liquid feed. When being grown in pots, either move it into a larger container in the summer or replace the top layers with new soil. Because growth will become quite straggly, give a light prune after flowering, which should stop it getting out of hand. Beware red spider mites and aphids.

OTHER VARIETIES *H. violacea* 'Happy Wanderer' (more vigorous, with mauve-purple flowers); *H. violacea* 'Pink Cascade' (pink flowers).

H

Haworthia cymbiformis

THIS FUN, QUIRKY, SMALL SOUTH AFRICAN SUCCULENT has thick, fleshy, pointed leaves with thin, pale green or greenish-white stripes. The leaves sometimes have a pink flush and eventually make such a packed cluster that it is hard to see where they are joined at the base. In spring, thin stems shoot up, carrying small, pinkish-white flowers. A good alternative is *H. pumila* (*see inset*), which has dark green or purple-green leaves liberally covered with white spots. Both are easy to grow and like fresh air, with moderate watering and a monthly, half-strength nitrogen liquid feed; keep dry over winter because they hate sitting in cold, wet soil. Beware mealybugs.

OTHER VARIETY *H. attenuata* (white marks on the long, thin, pointy leaves; white flowers).

PLANT PROFILE
HEIGHT 8cm (3in)
SPREAD 25cm (10in)
SITE Bright filtered light
SOIL Standard cactus compost
HARDINESS Min 10°C (50°F)
FLOWERING Spring

Hedera helix 'Eva' Common ivy

AN EXTREMELY USEFUL OUTDOOR PLANT, common ivy can also be grown in a hanging basket, pot or conservatory border, with the stems either trailing down or climbing up, supported on canes with horizontal wire set between them. Both methods show off the grey-green leaves with their creamy-white margins. All *H. helix* plants need to be well watered in full growth and given a monthly liquid feed; keep moist in winter. Give a trim at any time.

OTHER VARIETIES *H. helix* 'Bruder Ingobert' (leaves have creamy-white edging); *H. helix* 'Caecilia' (1m/3ft high, light green variegated leaves); *H. helix* 'Little Diamond' (30cm/12in high, grey-green variegated leaves); *H. helix* 'Perkeo' (45cm/18in high, dark green leaves with purple-tinted veins); *H. helix* 'Romanze' (light green leaves).

PLANT PROFILE	
HEIGHT	1.2m (4ft)
SITE	Bright indirect light
SOIL	John Innes No. 3
HARDINESS	Fully hardy

H | *Hedychium gardnerianum* Kahili ginger

ONE OF THE TOP TEN SCENTED FLOWERS for a conservatory, the Kahili ginger gives off a rich, spicy scent in late summer. Everything about it is exotic. The smartly upright stems show off its large leaves, which are up to 40cm (16in) long with a grey tinge, and the lemon-yellow flowers appear in a vertical, cylindrical-like cluster. It is much easier to grow than it looks, but some humidity is important. Water freely in the growing season and apply a monthly liquid feed. Over winter, keep it just moist. It can be placed outdoors over summer in a sheltered, lightly-shaded position. If planted outside in summer, provide rich, moist, free-draining soil; pot up again for the winter.

OTHER VARIETY *H. coronarium* (taller with large, white, richly-scented flowers).

PLANT PROFILE

HEIGHT 2m (6ft)

SPREAD 1m (3ft)

SITE Bright indirect light

SOIL John Innes No. 3

HARDINESS Half hardy

FLOWERING Late summer

Heliconia psittacorum Parrot's flower

RELATED TO THE LARGE-LEAVED BANANA TREES, heliconias have first-rate foliage and bright colours. Parrot's flower has leathery, rich green leaves about 30cm (12in) long with red stalks and, in summer, orange-red flowers. Its size, shape and colour make it a star conservatory plant, and it needs a big space where it can be clearly seen. If standing or planting it outside in early to midsummer (once the weather has warmed up), make sure it is sheltered from strong winds, which will ruin the leaves. Water freely when it is in full growth and apply a monthly liquid feed; water sparingly over winter. Beware red spider mites, mealybugs and snails.

OTHER VARIETY *H. rostrata* (potentially much taller, with red and yellow flowers; restrict size by growing it in a large pot).

PLANT PROFILE
HEIGHT 1.2m (4ft)
SPREAD 1.2m (4ft)
SITE Bright filtered light
SOIL For best results use a gritty orchid compost
HARDINESS Min 15°C (59°F)
FLOWERING Spring to summer

H

Heliotropium arborescens 'Marine'   Cherry pie

THE SUPERB, FRUITY SCENT (a bit like marzipan and vanilla), given off by its clusters of tiny, violet-blue flowers makes cherry pie one of the very best conservatory plants. A shrubby, leafy plant, it can be grown as a pot plant and trimmed to a rounded shape, planted in a conservatory border, or you can stand it outside over the summer in a sunny, sheltered position. Indoors, provide some humidity and shade from hot sun. Water moderately over summer and apply a monthly liquid feed; keep just moist in winter. It tends to be short-lived, but cuttings (taken from non-flowering shoots) easily root in summer to provide more plants. Protect against whiteflies.

OTHER VARIETIES *H.* 'Chatsworth' (mid-purple flowers, will reach 90cm/3ft high); *H.* 'White Lady (white flowers).

PLANT PROFILE

HEIGHT To 45cm (18in)

SPREAD To 45cm (18in)

SITE Full light

SOIL John Innes No. 3

HARDINESS Half hardy

FLOWERING Summer

Hemigraphis repanda

AN INTERESTING, LOW-GROWING MALAYSIAN EVERGREEN, the stems of *H. repanda* creep across the soil, creating a mat of 5cm (2in) long, thin leaves that are greyish-green with a red flush, sometimes with a purple hue. The colourful foliage provides an effective background for the white flowers, which appear from spring. The spreading growth means it is best suited to a conservatory border. Provide moderate to high humidity and water freely when in full growth, applying a monthly liquid feed; keep moist over winter. Established plants can be cut back in the spring to restrict their spread, but some of the flowers will be lost.

OTHER VARIETY *H.* 'Exotica' (the purple waffle plant has purple-green leaves and white flowers).

PLANT PROFILE
HEIGHT 23cm (9in)
SPREAD 45cm (18in)
SITE Bright filtered light
SOIL John Innes No. 3
HARDINESS 10°C (50°F)
FLOWERING Spring to summer

H

Hibbertia cuneiformis

A DISTINCTIVE, UNUSUAL SHRUB, *H. cuneiformis* tends to spread and will need plenty of space in a conservatory border. The freely-branching growth puts out small, bright green leaves about 2.5cm (1–2in) long and, from the end of winter, rich yellow flowers that make a bright show. To restrict its size and maintain a decent shape, give a light prune after flowering. Provide moderate humidity and water freely when in full growth, adding a monthly liquid feed; keep moist in winter. Coming from western Australia, it will tolerate hot, dry, desert-like conditions and even full shade.

OTHER VARIETY *H. volubilis* (more vigorous with larger, brighter summer flowers).

PLANT PROFILE
HEIGHT 1–2m (3–6ft)
SPREAD 1–1.5m (3–5ft)
SITE Bright filtered light
SOIL John Innes No. 2
HARDINESS Min 5°C (41°F)
FLOWERING Late winter to spring

Hibiscus rosa-sinensis 'Crown of Bohemia' Rose of China H

THIS LARGE, BUSHY EVERGREEN SHRUB has golden-yellow flowers that are flushed reddish-orange in the centre – they are nicely set off against a background of glossy, dark green leaves. Moderate humidity is important, as is good ventilation. Water freely over summer, applying a monthly liquid feed; water sparingly in winter. Long, hot summers invariably give the best results. Aphids, scale insects, mealybugs, whiteflies and powdery mildew may be a problem.

OTHER VARIETIES *H. rosa-sinensis* 'Agnes Galt' (pink flowers); *H. rosa-sinensis* 'Fiesta' (apricot-orange flowers); *H. rosa-sinensis* 'Kinchen's Yellow' (bright yellow flowers); *H. rosa-sinensis* 'The President' (rich red flowers).

PLANT PROFILE
HEIGHT 90cm (3ft)
SPREAD 60cm (24in)
SITE Bright filtered light
SOIL John Innes No. 2
HARDINESS Min 10–13°C (50–55°F)
FLOWERING Summer to autumn

H | *Hibiscus schizopetalus* Japanese lantern

A TERRIFIC PLANT FOR A LARGE CONSERVATORY, Japanese lantern is easy to look after and ought to be much more popular. An evergreen African shrub, it puts out long, slender, arching branches. They need to be tied into a system of horizontal wires fixed to a wall, or trained around posts so that the showy pink or red flowers – which are up to 8cm (3in) wide – can be clearly seen. Provide moderate humidity and good ventilation. Water freely over the summer, applying a monthly liquid feed; water sparingly in winter. Long, hot summers give the best results. Prone to aphids, scale insects, mealybugs, whiteflies and powdery mildew.

PLANT PROFILE

HEIGHT To 3m (10ft)

SPREAD 1–1.5m (3–5ft)

SITE Bright filtered light

SOIL John Innes No. 2

HARDINESS Min 10–13°C (50–55°F)

FLOWERING Summer

Hippeastrum 'Apple Blossom' Amaryllis

H

THESE BIG, SHOWY, FLAMBOYANT BULBS are perfect for a winter windowsill, and come in a wide range of colour from brash red to muted pastels – 'Apple Blossom' has large, white flowers with pink-tinged tips. Soak the roots in lukewarm water for 24 hours, then plant in a pot with the top half exposed above the surface. Stand in a warm position and water sparingly until there is active growth then water freely, adding a liquid feed every two weeks. After flowering, carry on watering, keeping the leaves green for two months; then water sparingly, stopping altogether when the leaves die down. Keep dry for 10–12 weeks, then begin gently watering.

OTHER VARIETIES *H.* 'Picotee' (white flowers, red rim); *H.* 'Red Sensation' (red flowers); *H.* 'Salmon Pink' (salmon pink flowers).

PLANT PROFILE
HEIGHT 30–50cm (12–20in)
SPREAD 30cm (12in)
SITE Full or bright filtered light
SOIL John Innes No. 2
HARDINESS Min 13°C (55°F)
FLOWERING Winter

H *Howea belmoreana* Sentry palm

THE EXCEPTIONALLY GRACEFUL SENTRY PALM has stems that shoot up and then gently arch over, where they extend into the base of the leaves. The leaves of older plants can well exceed 30cm (12in) long. *H. belmoreana* is slow growing and needs potting up only every three years. Shade from hot summer sun and occasionally mist to provide some humidity. Water moderately when in full growth, giving a monthly liquid feed; water sparingly in winter. Protect against red spider mites and scale insects.

OTHER VARIETY *H. forsteriana* (the kentia palm has slightly straighter leaves).

PLANT PROFILE
HEIGHT 2.4m (8ft)
SPREAD 1.2m (4ft)
SITE Full light
SOIL No. 2, with added peat substitute and leafmould
HARDINESS Min 7°C (45°F)

Hoya lanceolata subsp. *bella* Wax flower

H

SOME HOYAS ARE TALL CLIMBERS, but the considerably smaller wax flower is usually grown in a hanging basket (*see inset*). The downy stems with fleshy, rich green leaves are initially upright, but then they arch and dangle over the sides of the container. Alternatively, train the stems up and around a wire loop. Come summer, groups of seven to nine star-shaped white flowers with a red eye will appear, releasing a lovely sweet scent. Humid conditions are important. Water freely when in full growth, applying a monthly liquid feed. Keep moist in winter, but never let the soil become bone dry.

OTHER VARIETY *H. carnosa* (a taller climber that may reach 1.8m/6ft high, can be grown in a hanging basket; scented).

PLANT PROFILE

HEIGHT To 45cm (18in)

SPREAD To 45cm (18in)

SITE Bright filtered light

SOIL John Innes No. 2

HARDINESS Min 10°C (50°F)

FLOWERING Summer

H | *Hydrangea macrophylla* 'Blue Bonnet' Common hydrangea

THE COMMON HYDRANGEA is hardy enough to be grown outdoors, but it also makes a superb conservatory plant. For blue flowers, provide acid soil; pink flowers appear on alkaline soil. The dozens of varieties come in two categories: the mop-heads, (like 'Blue Bonnet') with rounded heads of flowers (typically used for pot plants), and the lacecaps with much flatter heads. Keep out of direct sun, and water well when in full growth, adding a tomato feed when the buds appear. After flowering, cut back the stems by half, keep watering, and stand in a cool greenhouse in summer, giving good ventilation; in late winter move indoors at 10°C (50°F).

OTHER VARIETY *H. macrophylla* 'Kluis Superba' (dark purple-blue to pink flowers).

PLANT PROFILE
HEIGHT 60cm (24in)
SPREAD 60cm (24in)
SITE Bright sun
SOIL Ericaceous (acid)
HARDINESS Fully hardy
FLOWERING Spring

Hypoestes phyllostachya Polka dot plant

H

A SHRUBBY, EVERGREEN, FOLIAGE PLANT from Madagascar, the polka dot plant is on the small side, but it is just right for growing in a pot or placing at the front of a conservatory border. The leaves give a show of dark green with a liberal scattering of white spots, and from late summer it bears tiny magenta to lilac flowers. To create an even more leafy and flowery fast-growing plant, nip out the growing tips in spring. Some humidity is important, as is liberal watering when in full growth, with a liquid feed every two to three weeks over summer; water sparingly in winter. Beware powdery mildew.

OTHER VARIETIES   *H. phyllostachya* 'Carmina' (bright red leaves); *H. phyllostachya* 'Purpurina' (purple leaves); Inset: *H. phyllostachya* 'Wit' (marbled leaves).

PLANT PROFILE

HEIGHT 30cm (12in)

SPREAD 23cm (9in)

SITE Bright filtered light

SOIL John Innes No. 2

HARDINESS Min 10°C (50°F)

FLOWERING Late summer to winter

I

Impatiens niamniamensis 'Congo Cockatoo' Busy Lizzie

THIS TENDER AFRICAN BUSY LIZZIE is a real eyecatcher with its brash yellow flowers and red spurs that resemble a parrot's bill. The effect is enlivened by the large, 20cm (8in) long, dark green leaves. 'Congo Cockatoo' is naturally bushy, but pinching out the growing tips in spring makes it even more so, and creates further flowers. Give it a prominent position on a conservatory table or place it to the front of a border where it can be clearly seen. Water moderately when in full growth, and apply a monthly liquid feed; water sparingly in winter. Prone to red spider mites, whiteflies and aphids.

OTHER VARIETY *I. repens* (for a hanging basket or to creep over the border soil, with yellow flowers).

PLANT PROFILE
HEIGHT 75cm (30in)
SPREAD 30cm (12in)
SITE Full to bright filtered light
SOIL John Innes No. 2
HARDINESS Min 15°C (59°F)
FLOWERING Summer

Iochroma cyaneum

I

THIS SOUTH AMERICAN SHRUB features groups of up to 20 tubular flowers that range in colour from deep purple to blue. Growth can be spreading or rather upright, with a nice covering of 5cm (2in) long, grey-green leaves that have a soft, hairy surface – also note the petal tips, which tend to curve back. Nip out the stem tips of young plants to make them even bushier. *I. cyaneum* takes up plenty of room and ideally needs a place in a conservatory border. Water moderately during full growth, and apply a monthly liquid feed; keep just moist in winter. Susceptible to red spider mites and whiteflies.

OTHER VARIETY *I. violaceum* (large clusters of violet-blue flowers).

PLANT PROFILE
HEIGHT 2m (6ft)
SPREAD 90cm (3ft)
SITE Bright to filtered light
SOIL John Innes No. 2
HARDINESS Min 7°C (45°F)
FLOWERING Summer

I *Iresine herbstii* 'Brilliantissima' Beefsteak plant

'BRILLIANTISSIMA' IS ONE OF THE BEST FOLIAGE PLANTS for a stunning dash of rich crimson. The 8cm (3in) long leaves, which have distinctive pink veins, stick out from stiffly upright stems. It is ideal for a conservatory border or pot, with contrasting, coloured plants placed behind and above. 'Brilliantissima' needs plenty of bright light or the rich red may fade and diminish – also nip out the growing points of the stems in spring to make the plants even leafier, giving more colour. Water well in the growing season, adding a monthly liquid feed; water sparingly over winter.

OTHER VARIETIES *I. herbstii* (look for forms with deep red or orange leaves); *I. herbstii* 'Wallisii' (dark purple-black leaves).

PLANT PROFILE
HEIGHT To 60cm (24in)
SPREAD To 50cm (20in)
SITE Full light
SOIL John Innes No. 2
HARDINESS Min 10°C (50°F)

Isolepis cernua Slender club-rush

I

SLENDER CLUB-RUSH GROWS IN THE WILD on peaty or sandy soil, sometimes near the coast in the UK, Europe and northern Africa. Its bright green mop of long, thin leaves should hang on all year given the protection of a conservatory. It is mainly used for its fun, rounded, architectural shape (*see inset*), which contrasts nicely with upright plants like the near black-leaved *Aeonium arboreum* 'Zwartkop' (*see page 22*). Only water when the compost surface (which needs added grit to make it free-draining) is dry; give a monthly liquid feed over summer and water sparingly in winter.

PLANT PROFILE

HEIGHT 15cm (6in)

SPREAD 45cm (18in)

SITE Bright to shady

SOIL John Innes No. 2

HARDINESS Min 7–10°C (45–50°F)

Isoplexis

FOUND GROWING IN THE WILD on the island of Tenerife, *Isoplexis* is a chunky bushy shrub with an increasingly spreading shape as it gets older. It is grown in conservatories for its deep green, 10cm (4in) long leaves, which are slightly hairy on the underside, and the tubular, bright orange-yellow, brownish-orange or yellow-brown flowers that appear in clusters. Water moderately when in full growth, applying a monthly liquid feed; water sparingly over winter. If it is placed outside in a pot over summer, provide a sheltered, sunny hot spot. Whiteflies and red spider mites may be a problem.

PLANT PROFILE

HEIGHT 1m (3½ft)

SPREAD 60cm (24in)

SITE Full or bright filtered light

SOIL John Innes No. 2

HARDINESS Min 5°C (41°F)

FLOWERING Summer

Ixora coccinea Flame of the woods

I

A BUSHY, ROUNDED INDIAN SHRUB, flame of the woods has the twin attractions of glossy, evergreen leaves and clusters of tiny red, orange, pink or yellow flowers, the red offering the most vivid show. Several different versions of this shrub have flowers in the same colour range – the red 'Superkings' are the smallest, at 1m (3ft) high. Keep it out of direct scorching sun and provide as much humidity as possible. Water freely when in full growth, but provide a sparing drink over winter. Each spring, replace the top layer of soil in the pot and add a slow-release fertilizer. Give a light spring prune to maintain a shapely look.

OTHER VARIETIES *I. coccinea* 'Jacqueline' (orange-red flowers - *see inset*); *I. coccinea* 'Orange King' (bright orange flowers).

PLANT PROFILE
HEIGHT 1.2–1.8m (4–6ft)
SPREAD 1.2m (4ft)
SITE Bright filtered light
SOIL Loamless potting compost
HARDINESS Min 15°C (59°F)
FLOWERING Early summer to autumn

J

Jaborosa integrifolia

ALTHOUGH IT CAN BE GROWN OUTSIDE in most gardens, given a sunny, sheltered spot, this South American perennial is well worth growing in a conservatory for its greenish-white flowers which release a lovely scent in the evenings. Being a notorious spreader, it can be used to pack a border with its short growth and dark green leaves, which make a colourful base beneath taller plants. Do not put anything small in its path or it will get swamped. Water moderately to well when in full growth, but less so when dormant over winter. Watch out for slugs.

PLANT PROFILE

HEIGHT 15cm (6in)

SPREAD Indefinite

SITE Bright light

SOIL Light and free-draining

HARDINESS Frost hardy

FLOWERING Summer

Jacaranda mimosifolia

J

A SENSATIONAL SOUTH AMERICAN TREE that can hit 15m (50ft) high in the wild, *J. mimosifolia* is much more restrained in a cool climate conservatory where it nonetheless puts on serious growth. The big attractions are the fern-like leaves and the early summer white-throated, purple-blue flowers. Ideally, grow it in a conservatory border (or failing that, in a large pot), giving it plenty of space. Prune moderately after flowering to maintain its shape and check its spread. Ventilate well and water freely when in full growth, adding a monthly liquid feed; water sparingly in winter. Beware whiteflies and red spider mites.

PLANT PROFILE

HEIGHT 3.6m (11ft)

SPREAD 2.7m (9ft)

SITE Full light

SOIL John Innes No. 3

HARDINESS Min 5–7°C (41–45°F)

FLOWERING Early summer

J | *Jasminum polyanthum* Jasmine

THE INDOOR JASMINE CAN EASILY FILL A ROOM with its fantastic scent. The only warning is that it eventually needs a big pot and will start twisting and twining every which way (*see inset*). Ideally, grow it in a border against a conservatory wall, where you can thread the bulk of its thin climbing stems up through a system of horizontal wires. Prune older stems right back after flowering to force up new vigorous shoots. Shade it from scorching sun and spray in hot weather. Water freely when in full growth and give a tomato liquid feed the moment the flower buds appear; water sparingly in winter. Keep on the cool side over winter. Prone to aphids and mealybugs.

OTHER VARIETY *J. sambac* (Arabian jasmine has dark green leaves and larger, scented white flowers that fade to pink).

PLANT PROFILE

HEIGHT To 3m (10ft)

SPREAD To 2m (6ft)

SITE Bright filtered light

SOIL John Innes No. 2

HARDINESS 7°C (45°F)

FLOWERING Late winter or early spring

Jatropha podagrica

J

OFTEN KNOWN AS THE GOUT PLANT, this low-growing, free-branching South American succulent is quite a curiosity. The stems emerge out of a short, swollen trunk and rarely have more than two to three very tough leaves at one time (*see inset*). Clusters of tiny red flowers, which take quite a while to open in succession, appear right at the stem tip. The key to success is warmth, without which there will not be any flowers. Make sure there is some shade from the hot summer sun and water moderately, adding a monthly liquid feed; keep completely dry in autumn and winter. If cutting back the stems, wear gloves, because the milky or watery latex can irritate the skin.

PLANT PROFILE
HEIGHT 50cm (20in) or more
SPREAD 25cm (10in)
SITE Full light
SOIL John Innes No. 2
HARDINESS Min 10°C (50°F)
FLOWERING Summer

J

Juanulloa mexicana

A SOUTH AMERICAN EVERGREEN SHRUB that tends to grow all over the place, *J. mexicana* produces small clusters of highly unusual orange flowers. They provide a nice contrast with the 15cm (6in) long, leathery leaves, which are woolly on the underside. Nip out the tips of young plants in the spring to make them bushier, and prune after flowering to give a better shape. Also insert canes to support the stems and help show off the flowers. Add some horticultural sand and grit to the soil to improve drainage and shade from the hot summer sun. Water moderately and apply a monthly liquid feed – it needs average to low humidity. Water sparingly in winter. Red spider mites and mealybugs may be a problem.

PLANT PROFILE

HEIGHT 1.2m (4ft)

SPREAD 75cm (30in)

SITE Full light

SOIL John Innes No. 2

HARDINESS Min 13°C (55°F)

FLOWERING Summer

Justicia brandegeeana Shrimp plant

A BUSHY EVERGREEN SHRUB, the shrimp plant puts on masses of leafy growth and has a good covering of peculiar, salmon-coloured flowers – about 10cm (4in) long – with a white tongue popping out of the open mouth. Plants generally need a hard annual pruning to stop them from getting out of hand. They will eventually develop a bare portion at the base, although they can easily be replaced with cuttings taken in the spring. Provide average to high humidity, and water well when in full growth with a monthly liquid feed; keep just moist in winter. Susceptible to red spider mites and whiteflies.

OTHER VARIETIES *J. brandegeeana* 'Yellow Queen' (bright yellow flowers); *J. carnea* (rosy-pink flowers).

PLANT PROFILE

HEIGHT To 1m (3ft)

SPREAD To 1m (3ft)

SITE Bright filtered light

SOIL John Innes No. 2 or 3

HARDINESS Min 7°C (45°F)

FLOWERING Intermittently all year

J *Justicia carnea* Brazilian plume

A SHOWY, EVERGREEN SOUTH AMERICAN SHRUB, the Brazilian plume has a good combination of large leaves – about 20cm (8in) long – and dense clusters of light pink flowers at the tips of the stems (*see inset*). Prune quite hard into the old growth in late winter or early spring for bushier and more flowery growth, and to restrict its size. Stand it in a draught-free position with shade from hot summer sun, and provide decent humidity. Water freely when in full growth, applying a liquid feed once a month; keep just moist in winter. If plants become shapeless and straggly, replace with cuttings taken in late spring or midsummer. Beware red spider mites and whiteflies.

PLANT PROFILE

HEIGHT 1.2m (4ft)

SPREAD 75cm (30in)

SITE Bright filtered light

SOIL John Innes No. 2 or 3

HARDINESS Min 7°C (45°F)

FLOWERING Summer and autumn

Justicia rizzinii

J

AN EVERGREEN BRAZILIAN SHRUB, *J.rizzinii* is small enough to be grown in a pot where it gives plenty of winter colour with its thin, tube-like, red flowers that turn yellow towards the rim. It is also extremely useful for perking up gaps in a conservatory border. Nip out the shoot tips of young plants at the start of the growing season (using these cuttings to provide another batch of plants) to make them bushier and much more flowery. Provide average to high humidity, and water well in full growth, adding a monthly liquid feed; keep just moist in winter. Red spider mites and whiteflies may be a problem.

PLANT PROFILE

HEIGHT To 60cm (24in)

SPREAD 30–60cm (12–24in)

SITE Bright filtered light

SOIL John Innes No. 2 or 3

HARDINESS Min 7°C (45°F)

FLOWERING Autumn to late spring

K | *Kalanchoe beharensis*

THE SIZE OF THE SUPERB, VELVET-LIKE, almost triangular leaves of *K. beharensis*, which may reach 15cm (6in) long, explains why it is popularly called elephants ears. The usually concave leaves, olive to brown on top and silvery beneath, are covered by fine silver or golden hairs. It quickly makes an impressive, bushy pot plant but the tiny yellow-green flowers will only appear on established plants. The soil needs added horticultural sand or grit to make it much more free-draining. Provide moderate watering over summer, with a liquid feed on three to four occasions; keep just moist in winter. Protect against mealybugs, aphids and mildew.

OTHER VARIETY *K. dagoensis* (equally spectacular, with a starburst of small leaves at the end of each stem).

PLANT PROFILE
HEIGHT 1m (3ft)
SPREAD 1m (3ft)
SITE Bright filtered light
SOIL John Innes No. 2
HARDINESS Min 10°C (50°F)
FLOWERING Late winter or early spring

Kalanchoe blossfeldiana Flaming katy

K

THIS EYE-CATCHING, BUSY LITTLE PLANT has fleshy dark green leaves, sometimes with a thin red rim, and brash clusters of tiny red flowers (*see inset*). Other varieties are available in a range of colours, including white, yellow, and pink. The soil needs added horticultural sand or grit to make it free-draining. It is quite happy in a dry, centrally-heated atmosphere, or on a sunny windowsill, and only needs moderate watering over summer, with a liquid feed on three to four occasions. Keep just moist in winter. It can be made to flower all year (after which it is best discarded) by giving it artificially long nights in summer with over 12 hours of darkness. Vulnerable to mealybugs, aphids and mildew.

OTHER VARIETIES *K.* hybrids (available in different colours).

PLANT PROFILE
HEIGHT To 40cm (16in)
SPREAD To 40cm (16in)
SITE Bright filtered light
SOIL John Innes No. 2
HARDINESS Min 12°C (54°F)
FLOWERING Early spring

K | *Kalanchoe daigremontiana* Mexican hat plant

A BIZARRE LITTLE MADAGASCAN SUCCULENT, the Mexican hat plant has eye-catching, 15cm (6in) long leaves, usually with reddish-brown spots, that stick out from an upright stem. Note that the leaves are toothed around the edges, which is where new plantlets appear (gardening books call them 'adventitious', which means that they appear in unusual places). The winter flowers are greyish-violet. The soil needs added horticultural sand or grit to make it free-draining. Provide moderate watering over summer, with a liquid feed on three to four occasions; keep just moist in winter. Prone to mealybugs, aphids and mildew.

OTHER VARIETY *K. tomentosa* (grey leaves with furry silver hairs, grows about 45cm/18in high).

PLANT PROFILE

HEIGHT 1m (3ft)

SPREAD 30cm (12in)

SITE Bright filtered light

SOIL John Innes No. 2

HARDINESS Min 10°C (50°F)

FLOWERING Winter

Kalanchoe fedtschenkoi 'Variegata'

AN EXCELLENT, MEDIUM-SIZED SUCCULENT POT PLANT, 'Variegata' has blue-green leaves – sometimes flushed pink and mottled yellow – with wavy edges and attractive creamy-white margins. In summer, it bears dangling, bell-shaped red or purple flowers. It prefers soil that has been made relatively open and free-draining by mixing in handfuls of horticultural sand or grit. Water moderately over the summer, with a liquid feed on three to four occasions; keep just moist in winter. Susceptible to mealybugs, aphids and mildew.

OTHER VARIETY *K. fedtschenkoi* (without the variegated markings and wavy edges on the leaves).

PLANT PROFILE

HEIGHT 50cm (20in)

SPREAD 50cm (20in)

SITE Bright filtered light

SOIL John Innes No. 2

HARDINESS Min 10°C (50°F)

FLOWERING Summer

K

Kalanchoe 'Wendy'

A BEAUTIFULLY-COLOURED KALANCHOE, 'Wendy' has a good show of small, downward-pointing, bell-shaped flowers. They are purple-red with orange or yellow right around the lip of the mouth, and appear at the end of winter. The plants tend to have dangling to semi-erect stems, covered by glossy green leaves up to 7cm (3in) long, which makes them a good choice for a hanging basket. The soil needs added horticultural sand or grit to make it free-draining. Water moderately over summer with a liquid feed on three to four occasions; keep just moist in winter. Beware mealybugs, aphids and mildew.

OTHER VARIETY *K.* 'Tessa' (strong spreader, with dangling orange-red flowers).

PLANT PROFILE

HEIGHT 30cm (12in)

SPREAD 30cm (12in)

SITE Bright filtered light

SOIL John Innes No. 2

HARDINESS Min 10°C (50°F)

FLOWERING Late winter and early spring

Kohleria digitaliflora

K

THIS COLOMBIAN PLANT has an attractive mix of 20cm (8in) long dark green leaves with paler markings and, in summer, tiny foxglove-like flowers. The flowers have a purple-pink body (covered in fine hairs, just like the leaves) with exquisite white lips and dark spots. If the plant becomes straggly, cut it back after flowering to prompt plenty of fresh new growth. Provide high humidity, and water moderately with rain- or soft water at first, then more freely when in full growth. When the flower buds appear, apply a liquid tomato feed every two weeks. Keep virtually dry over winter.

OTHER VARIETY *K. eriantha* (larger at 1m/3ft high, with tubular orange-red flowers over summer).

PLANT PROFILE
HEIGHT 60cm (24in)
SPREAD 45cm (18in)
SITE Bright filtered light
SOIL Loamless potting compost
HARDINESS Min 15°C (59°F)
FLOWERING Summer to autumn

L

Lachenalia aloides Cape cowslip

THIS SOUTH AFRICAN COWSLIP, nothing like the traditional
European kind, often has mottled stems that are red at the top.
Towards the end of winter, it bears tubular yellow flowers with red
lips. The leaves, with their sprinkling of purple spots, add to the
excellent show. Try Cape cowslips in pots or in the border of an
unheated conservatory. Only moderate watering is required until it
is in full growth – at this point, give it more regular drinks, with an
added liquid feed every 10 to 14 days. As the leaves fade, reduce
watering, and keep dry until fresh growth starts in the autumn.

OTHER VARIETIES   *L. aloides* 'Nelsonii' (golden-yellow flowers, but
the leaves lack spots); *L. aloides* 'Pearsonii' (apricot flowers).

PLANT PROFILE

HEIGHT 15–30cm
(6–12in)

SPREAD 5cm (2in)

SITE Full light

SOIL John Innes No. 2

HARDINESS Half hardy

FLOWERING Winter or
early spring

Leea coccinea 'Burgundy' West Indian holly

L

THIS BURMESE SHRUB IS WIDELY SEEN in gardens in the West Indies – it has sprays of burgundy-red leaves, the best colour being on the new spring growth. It must be treated with care or the leaves (which are more impressive than the small, pink summer flowers) will promptly fall. Also make sure that plants are kept at a constant temperature in a draught-free position, and avoid the temptation to water more than strictly necessary, especially over winter. Provide moderate humidity, water regularly when in full growth and apply a monthly liquid feed; water sparingly when dormant. Protect against red spider mites.

OTHER VARIETY *L. coccinea* (similar but with bronze young leaves that gradually turn glossy green).

PLANT PROFILE
HEIGHT 1.2m (4ft)
SPREAD 1m (3ft)
SITE Bright filtered light
SOIL John Innes No. 3
HARDINESS Min 16°C (61°F)
FLOWERING Summer

L | *Lithops salicola* Living stones

ODD AND MINISCULE, these grey South African succulents, or
living stones, are perfectly camouflaged against the stony ground.
The upright parts of the plant are actually two united swollen leaves
that produce, after the intense summer heat of the semi-desert
regions where they grow, pure white, daisy-like flowers (*see inset*).
Other similar lithops (invariably shorter and better camouflaged) are
available with patterned tops. Water freely from early summer to late
autumn, adding a weak monthly liquid feed; avoid any temptation
to water at other times when it is dormant.

OTHER VARIETY   *L. pseudotruncatella* var. *pulmonuncula* (tiny 'stones'
that produce flashy yellow flowers).

PLANT PROFILE

HEIGHT 5cm (2in)

SPREAD 23cm (9in)

SITE Full light

SOIL Standard cactus
compost

HARDINESS Min 12°C
(54°F)

FLOWERING Late summer
to mid-autumn

Livistona chinensis Chinese fan palm

L

THE BASE OF THE CHINESE FAN PALM is a swollen piece of trunk with slender vertical stems above it and plenty of glossy, rich green leaves divided into long thin strips. In summer, it produces small seed pods. Do not be alarmed by its vigorous statistics in the Far East, where it may reach 12m (40ft) high, because when grown in a pot, in north-west Europe, it will be much more restrained. Restrict the height even more by keeping it in a medium-size container, only repotting every five years or so when the health of the plant demands it. Water freely in the growing season, adding a monthly liquid feed; water sparingly over winter.

PLANT PROFILE

HEIGHT 2m (6ft)

SPREAD 2m (6ft)

SITE Full light

SOIL John Innes No. 3

HARDINESS Min 3–5°C (37–41°F)

L | *Lotus berthelotii* Parrot's beak

A WONDERFULLY EXOTIC TRAILING plant for a hanging basket, parrot's beak looks terrific and is extremely easy to grow. The long, thin dangling stems have an array of thin, silvery, ornamental leaves and, in late spring, orange-red to scarlet, black-centred, beak-like flowers. Some pruning may be necessary after flowering to keep the rampant growth in check. It may be placed outside for the summer, but bring back indoors in early autumn. Parrot's beak only needs a cool winter conservatory to thrive, with free-draining compost (add horticultural grit), as well as liberal watering in summer with a monthly liquid feed; keep just moist in winter.

OTHER VARIETY *L. maculatus* (similar but with red- or orange-tipped yellow flowers).

PLANT PROFILE

HEIGHT 20cm (8in)

SPREAD 90cm (3ft)

SITE Full light

SOIL John Innes No. 2

HARDINESS Half hardy (borderline)

FLOWERING Spring and early summer

L

Lotus hirsutus Hairy canary clover

A HARDY MEDITERRANEAN SHRUBBY PLANT, hairy canary clover makes a valuable evergreen specimen for a conservatory border or pot. The creamy-white flowers appear at the tips of the stems over a long period, and are followed by reddish-brown seed pods. Stand outside over the summer months because it likes fresh air, or ventilate the conservatory well, and make sure that the soil has added grit to provide good drainage. Water freely when in full growth, giving a monthly liquid feed, but water sparingly in winter because when dormant wet soil can be fatal. Prone to mealybugs, aphids and red spider mites.

PLANT PROFILE

HEIGHT 45cm (18in)

SPREAD 60cm (24in)

SITE Full light

SOIL John Innes No. 2 with added grit

HARDINESS -10°C (0°F)

FLOWERING Summer to early autumn

L

Lytocaryum weddellianum Weddell palm

THE EXTRAORDINARY, SLENDER-STEMMED WEDDELL PALM will never become too big for a conservatory – initially as wide as a thumb, it only grows a few centimetres a year. Each leaf consists of small narrow leaflets that are bright green on top and greyish-green beneath. When it is about 10 years old, it should begin to produce cup-shaped, three-petalled green flowers in summer. Some catalogues call it the miniature coconut palm, but instead of coconuts, you actually get tiny fruit, and then only if you have separate male and female plants. Water moderately when in full growth, giving a monthly liquid feed; water sparingly over winter.

PLANT PROFILE

HEIGHT 2m (6ft)

SPREAD 1m (3ft))

SITE Full light

SOIL John Innes No. 2

HARDINESS Min 13°C (55°F)

FLOWERING Summer

Mammillaria hahniana Old lady cactus

M

SOME OF THE MOST INTERESTING MAMILLARIAS have white, furry fuzzy hair covering their heavily-spined little bodies. In the case of *M. hahniana*, this helps set off the tiny purple-red flowers, which appear in rings around the crown and are followed by red seed pods (*see inset*). Old lady cactus is easy to look after – for aesthetic reasons and to facilitate fast drainage, grow it in a pot with small pebbles on the soil surface. Shade plants from the hot summer sun, provide low levels of humidity, and water freely from mid-spring to autumn, adding a monthly liquid feed from late spring. Water sparingly over winter, when excess amounts can be fatal.

OTHER VARIETIES *M. magnimamma* (pink to purple flowers, often nasty spines); *M. parkinsonii* (red flowers, white spines with black tips).

PLANT PROFILE

HEIGHT To 20cm (8in)

SPREAD To 40cm (16in)

SITE Full light

SOIL Standard cactus compost

HARDINESS Min 7–10°C (45–50°F)

FLOWERING Spring to summer

M | *Mandevilla* x *amabilis* 'Alice du Pont'

A FUN SOUTH AMERICAN CLIMBER with woody stems, 'Alice du Pont' adds a jungly, exotic touch with its large, thick, shiny green leaves and succession of pink flowers that bloom through the summer. It should be grown up against a set of horizontal wires on a wall to show off the dark-throated flowers – young plants can be initially grown up a cane in a pot. Prune after flowering by nipping back the sideshoots on the main branches, leaving three to four buds. Shade from hot sun, and water moderately in the growing season, giving a monthly liquid feed; water sparingly in winter. Beware red spider mites, whiteflies and mealybugs.

OTHER VARIETY *M. laxa* (the Chilean jasmine grows about 3.6m/12ft high, with nicely-scented white flowers).

PLANT PROFILE

HEIGHT To 3m (10ft)

SITE Full light

SOIL John Innes No. 3

HARDINESS Min 10–15°C (50–59°F)

FLOWERING Summer

Manettia luteorubra Brazilian firecracker

M

A MODEST, SOUTH AMERICAN, EVERGREEN TWINING-CLIMBER, it gets its firecracker name because it has a profusion of small, bright red, tubular flowers, each with an eye-catching yellow mouth, which stand out well against the background of green leaves. Grow it up a set of horizontal wall wires, or tie it to a group of canes. Prune after flowering by nipping back the sideshoots on the main branches, leaving about three to four buds. Provide decent humidity, and water moderately with a monthly liquid feed in the growing season; water sparingly in winter. Protect against whiteflies.

OTHER VARIETY *M. inflata* (similar climber, also with red flowers and a yellow mouth).

PLANT PROFILE

HEIGHT 2m (6ft)

SITE Bright filtered light

SOIL John Innes No. 2

HARDINESS Min 7°C (45°F)

FLOWERING Summer

M

Maranta leuconeura var. *kerchoveana* Rabbit's foot

THE MARANTAS ARE GROWN for their beautifully-patterned foliage, but are tricky to keep because they are used to life in humid South American rainforests, deep beneath the leafy canopy. Rabbit's foot has light grey-green leaves (blue-grey underneath) that fold up at night – they also have what look like purple-brown rabbit footprint's running up the center. Remove the buds because the flowers are insignificant. Because the root system is not very deep, provide a wide, shallow container, and maintain high humidity at all times. Water moderately in full growth, adding a monthly liquid feed; water sparingly in winter. Prone to red spider mites.

OTHER VARIETY *M. leuconeura* var. *erythroneura* (green leaves have bold red veins, with pale green marks up the centre).

PLANT PROFILE
HEIGHT 30cm (12in)
SPREAD 30cm (12in)
SITE Bright indirect light
SOIL John Innes No. 2
HARDINESS Min 15°C (59°F)
FLOWERING Summer

Medinilla magnifica

M

ONE OF THE MOST EXTRAORDINARY flowering conservatory plants, this evergreen from the Philippines produces a long stem with a kind of parachute of large petals at the end and, tucked up beneath, dozens of tiny pink flowers (*see inset*). Though the overall growth is not that big, the leaves are glossy, leathery and upstanding, giving an exotic touch. Grow it in a pot perched up high, perhaps on top of a pillar so that you can look up at the descending flowers. Keep out of hot, direct sun and provide high humidity. Water moderately when in full growth, adding a monthly liquid feed; water sparingly in winter. Scale insects may be a problem.

PLANT PROFILE

HEIGHT 1m (3ft)

SPREAD 1m (3ft)

SITE Bright filtered light

SOIL John Innes No. 2

HARDINESS Min 15°C (59°F)

FLOWERING Spring to summer

M | *Mimosa pudica* Sensitive plant

THIS IS THE TROPICAL PLANT that children have to be kept well away from because it is such good fun to touch (*see inset*). Poke the thin leaves, even ever so lightly, and they promptly fold shut and will not open again for about one hour. The tiny lilac to light pink flowers open in the summer. Do not expect the sensitive plant to live for a long time, especially if it is being constantly tapped and stroked, but replacements can be readily bought or easily grown from seed in the spring. Shade from hot sun, and water moderately in the growing season, when it needs a monthly liquid feed; water sparingly in winter.

PLANT PROFILE

HEIGHT 30–45cm (12–18in)

SPREAD 40cm (16in)

SITE Full light

SOIL John Innes No. 2

HARDINESS Min 13°C (55°F)

FLOWERING Summer

Monstera deliciosa 'Variegata' Swiss cheese plant

M

GROWN WELL, THIS CONSERVATORY CLICHÉ is a superb plant with whacking great glossy leaves with creamy markings that look like they have been vigorously chewed. It needs support (even in the wild its aerial roots need to cling onto supporting structures) in the shape of a stout moss pole, which needs to be regularly sprayed to provide some humidity (*see inset*). If growth gets too high and vigorous, prune it back in the spring, whereupon a new leading shoot will emerge from high up the stem. Do not be surprised if 'Variegata' reverts to all green. Water freely when in full growth, applying a monthly liquid feed; water sparingly in winter. Protect against scale insects and red spider mites.

OTHER VARIETY *M. deliciosa* (without the creamy markings).

PLANT PROFILE	
HEIGHT 3m (10ft)	
SPREAD 1.5m (5ft)	
SITE Bright indirect light	
SOIL John Innes No. 2	
HARDINESS Min 15°C (59°F)	
FLOWERING Spring to summer	

M | *Musa basjoo* Japanese banana

IT CAN BE GROWN OUTDOORS ALL YEAR, but the Japanese banana needs a mild, sunny, sheltered garden and must be wrapped up over winter with straw to protect it against the cold. A safer bet is to keep it in the conservatory, possibly standing it outside over summer (note that the large leaves will get flayed if exposed to strong winds). It takes a few years to flower, whereupon the main trunk dies back and is replaced by the new growth at its base, eventually creating a multi-stemmed plant (slice off unwanted shoots). Ultimately, it needs a 60cm (24in) pot. Water freely over summer, applying a monthly liquid feed; keep just moist in winter.

OTHER VARIETY *M. acuminata* 'Dwarf Cavendish' (the small version at 1m/3ft high, but it lacks those whopping big leaves).

PLANT PROFILE	
HEIGHT	2.5m (8ft)
SPREAD	1.2m (4ft)
SITE	Full light
SOIL	John Innes No. 3
HARDINESS	Frost hardy
FLOWERING	Summer

Nematanthus 'Tropicana'

SOME OF THE MORE POPULAR Brazilian nematanthus are trailing plants for a hanging basket, but this is a multi-branching shrubby plant with two main attractions – the thick, fleshy, glossy, dark green leaves on purple stems, and the dark yellow flowers that appear at intervals throughout the year. Nip out the tips of the growing shoots in spring to create a bushier plant. Shield from hot sun and water moderately with rain- or soft water over summer, adding a monthly liquid feed; give a more sparing drink in winter. The best way to get winter flowers is to maintain a temperature of 15–16°C (59–61°F). Beware aphids on new growth.

OTHER VARIETIES *N.* 'Freckles' (trailing plant with red spots on yellow flowers); *N. gregarius* (bright orange flowers; can trail).

PLANT PROFILE	
HEIGHT 30cm (12in)	
SPREAD 45cm (18in)	
SITE Bright filtered light	
SOIL Loamless potting compost	
HARDINESS Min 13°C (55°F)	
FLOWERING Intermittently all year	

N | *Neoregelia concentrica*

THE SHOWY NEOREGELIAS ARE GROWN for their superb rosette of leaves. In the case of *N. concentrica*, these leaves are often attractively marked dark purple right at the tips, with black spines along the edges of the leaves. In summer, the yellow-white cup in the centre of the rosette turns purple-pink, with blue or white flowers emerging from it. Water freely when in growth, using rain- or soft water, and apply a diluted nitrogen feed from spring to late autumn. Keep the central cup topped up with water. Scale insects may be a problem.

OTHER VARIETY *N. carolinae* (the central leaves turn bright red in summer when the blue flowers appear – *see inset*).

PLANT PROFILE
HEIGHT To 30cm (12in)
SPREAD To 70cm (28in)
SITE Bright filtered light
SOIL Epiphytic compost
HARDINESS Min 10°C (50°F)
FLOWERING Summer

Nepenthes x hookerinana

THE CLIMBING TENDRILS of *N. x hookerinana* – which reach 3m (10ft) high in Borneo – put out hanging, elongated, nectar-filled pouches that trap insects inside. They slip down into a liquid bath where they decompose and provide a nourishing 'soup'. The largest nepenthes have apparently caught small birds and rats. Provide high humidity and a minimum of 15°C (59°F) on winter nights and 21°C (70°F) on summer nights. Prune mature plants in spring by two-thirds to promote more 'pitchers', and provide a weekly, high-nitrogen liquid feed over summer. Water regularly all year, but never to excess.

OTHER VARIETIES *N. mirabilis* (strong grower with long 'pitchers'); *N. rafflesiana* (easily-grown straggly climber).

PLANT PROFILE

HEIGHT 1.2m (4ft)

SITE Bright filtered light

SOIL Carnivorous plant compost

HARDINESS Min (daytime) 24°C (75°F)

FLOWERING Summer

N *Nephrolepis exaltata* 'Bostoniensis' **Boston fern**

A THOROUGHLY RELIABLE MOUND of foliage with an array of outward-pointing, fresh green fronds, the Boston fern makes an ideal gap filler in the border. It can also be grown amongst a display of pot plants or in a hanging basket where its divided leaves (which is why it is also called the ladder fern) can be clearly seen (*see inset*). Provide ventilation and some humidity because if the atmosphere gets too hot and dry, the leaf tips will turn brown and ruin the look. Water moderately when in full growth using rain- or soft water, and add a monthly, half-strength liquid feed; water sparingly in winter.

OTHER VARIETY *N. exaltata* (slightly more narrow leaves).

PLANT PROFILE

HEIGHT To 60cm (24in)

SPREAD To 60cm (24in)

SITE Bright filtered light

SOIL 1 part loam, 2 parts sharp sand, 3 parts leafmould

HARDINESS Min 7–10°C (45–50°F)

Nerium oleander Rose bay, Oleander

THIS SMALL FLOWERING MEDITERRANEAN TREE is easily grown as a shrubby plant in a pot or conservatory border. It has a nice combination of thin, pointy, evergreen leaves and typically pink (possibly red or white) flowers that appear in the spring and can continue into the autumn. Prune hard in late winter to restrict size and prompt new vigorous growth (wear gloves because it is toxic and skin contact can trigger a bad reaction). Water moderately in full growth, giving a monthly liquid feed, when it can also be stood outside because it likes plenty of fresh air. Water sparingly in winter. Beware scale insects, mealybugs and red spider mites.

OTHER VARIETIES *N. oleander* 'Petite Pink' (half as high with pink flowers); *N. oleander* 'Variegatum' (whitish-edged leaves, pink flowers).

PLANT PROFILE

HEIGHT 2m (6ft)

SPREAD 1m (3ft)

SITE Full light

SOIL John Innes No. 3

HARDINESS Min 2–5°C (36–41°F)

FLOWERING Summer

N

Nertera granadensis Bead plant

THIS TINY FLAMBOYANT PLANT from Central America and Mexico looks perfectly innocuous in early summer, when it has just a low mound of bright green leaves. Shortly after this, it is liberally covered by small, yellowish-green flowers, which are then followed by a colourful eruption of shiny orange or bright red berries. The bead plant is extremely easy to grow and makes a bright display when placed on a windowsill while the berries are out (*see inset*). When in full growth, water freely by standing the pot in a tray filled with water (apply a monthly liquid feed in the same way); water sparingly over winter. Protect against aphids and red spider mites.

PLANT PROFILE

HEIGHT 2cm (¾in)

SPREAD 15cm (6in)

SITE Bright filtered light

SOIL Loamless potting compost

HARDINESS Half hardy

FLOWERING Summer

Nidularium regeliodes Bird's nest bromeliad

THE BIRD'S NEST BROMELIAD from southern Brazil provides a smart colour contrast with bright green leaves and striking red bracts that surround the clusters of five to eight tubular red flowers. It is impossible to predict when the flowers will appear and, although it should be over summer, they may occasionally open at other times. Provide moderate to high humidity by misting with soft water in the early morning; water freely with rain- or soft water during the growing season. Apply a diluted nitrogen feed each month, from spring to late autumn, ensuring the rosettes then stay filled with soft water. Keep plants just moist in winter.

OTHER VARIETY *N. procerum* (up to 75cm/30in wide, with copper-tinged, pale green leaves, and blue-tipped red flowers).

PLANT PROFILE
HEIGHT 30cm (12in)
SPREAD 40cm (18in)
SITE Bright filtered light
SOIL Epiphytic bromeliad compost
HARDINESS Min 12°C (54°F)
FLOWERING Summer

N | *Nolinia recurvata* Bottle palm, Elephant foot tree

THIS BIZARRE, MEXICAN PLANT has a long bare leg of a stem topped by a whirligig of long, thin leaves. The base of the plant resembles an onion bulging out of the soil and acts as a water reservoir (*see inset*), which means the plant will not suffer if you occasionally forget to water it. The pot should be on the small side, and can be placed outside over summer. After watering, let the soil in the top half of the pot dry out, then give it another drink; water sparingly in winter. If the leaf tips turn brown in a dry atmosphere, just give them a trim and mist over the plant to make sure it does not happen again. Susceptible to red spider mites. It is still known and sometimes sold as *Beaucarnea recurvata*.

PLANT PROFILE

HEIGHT 2.4m (8ft)

SPREAD 1.2m (4ft)

SITE Full light

SOIL John Innes No. 2

HARDINESS Min 7°C (45°F)

FLOWERING Summer

Nopalxochia ackermannii

EASILY-GROWN NOPALXOCHIA CACTI come from southern Mexico and Central America, and provide a wide range of flower colours, including exquisite lilac-pink and bright red. *N. ackermannii* has flat, thin, fleshy stems that bear open, crimson or orange-red flowers with pale yellow-green tubes, which last for three to four days and close up at night. Provide moderate humidity by standing the pot in a large pebble-filled plastic saucer, with rain- or soft water just about reaching the surface of the stones. Avoid draughts, and water freely over summer, applying a diluted liquid feed each month. Keep barely moist from late autumn to late winter.

OTHER VARIETIES *N.* 'Celestine' (reddish-pink flowers); *N.* 'Gloria' (red to pink flowers); *N.* 'Zoe' (peach-orange flowers).

PLANT PROFILE

HEIGHT 45cm (18in)

SPREAD 40cm (16in)

SITE Bright, filtered light

SOIL Slightly acid, epiphytic cactus compost

HARDINESS Min 10°C (50°F)

FLOWERING Late spring or early summer

O

Odontoglossum crispum

THIS EVERGREEN ORCHID is easy to grow in relatively cool conditions. It produces showy white winter flowers, often with a highly attractive splattering of yellow and red in the centre, which last about six weeks. Other kinds of odontoglossum are even more brightly patterned. While this one is not a prima donna, it does need specific requirements. Keep the summer temperature under 24°C (75°F), ventilate well and provide good humidity. Water freely – keeping the compost moist – using rain- or soft water over summer, adding an orchid feed every third watering; water sparingly in winter. Prone to red spider mites, aphids and mealybugs.

OTHER VARIETY *O.* Marie Noel 'Bourgogyne' (an elaborately-patterned orchid with red marks on a white background).

PLANT PROFILE
HEIGHT 30cm (12in)
SPREAD 30cm (12in)
SITE Bright filtered light
SOIL Epiphytic orchid compost
HARDINESS Min 10°C (50°F)
FLOWERING Winter

Olea europaea Olive

THIS TREE WILL PRODUCE FRESH OLIVES in a conservatory but it must have a cold winter and a long, hot summer in order to flower and fruit. The tiny, scented, yellow summer flowers are a good attraction, but the bitter autumn olives – not as tasty as the ones in the Mediterranean – need to be pickled in brine before eating. All olive trees are self-fertile, but there will be a larger crop on each if more trees are grown together – those listed below give the best results. Water moderately during the growing season, providing a monthly liquid feed, when it may also be placed outside. Water sparingly in winter. Beware scale insects.

OTHER VARIETIES *O. europaea* 'Aglandau' (reliably hardy); *O.europaea* 'Cailletier' (quite hardy).

PLANT PROFILE
HEIGHT To 3m (10ft)
SPREAD To 2m (6ft)
SITE Full light
SOIL John Innes No. 3 with added sharp sand
HARDINESS -5°C (23°F)
FLOWERING Summer

O *Oplismenus africanus* 'Variegatus'

OFTEN CALLED BASKET GRASS, 'Variegatus' resembles a tradescantia (*see pp. 305–6*) because of its long, thin, pointy green leaves – often tinged purple-pink – with white stripes. It is best grown in a hanging basket with the leaves tumbling over the sides, or as ground cover to pile up in a conservatory border. Because its parent plant comes from tropical forests, it needs plenty of bright, filtered light. Water well over summer, applying a monthly liquid feed, and do not let the soil dry out; water sparingly in winter. It is sometimes listed in catalogues as *O. africanus* 'Vittatus'.

OTHER VARIETY *O. africanus* (plain green leaves).

PLANT PROFILE
HEIGHT 90cm (3ft)
SPREAD Indefinite
SITE Bright filtered or full light
SOIL John Innes No. 2
HARDINESS Min 5°C (41°F)
FLOWERING Summer to winter

Opuntia santa-rita

O

THIS IS ONE OF THE FINEST OPUNTIAS, but it comes in different forms, so look before you buy. Many have blue-grey pads with a lovely purple flush, and the flowers appear in early summer. The degree to which it will have spines (all with a nasty barbed top) does vary, but even the little ones are a terrible nuisance if you get one in your skin, and it will be like extracting a splinter. Coming from desert regions, it needs free-draining soil (add grit to the compost) and moderate watering over summer, with a quarter-dose monthly feed from spring to midsummer. Let the compost dry out between watering; keep it bone dry in winter.

OTHER VARIETY *O. robusta* (a chunkier, more robust plant that grows 2m/6ft high).

PLANT PROFILE
HEIGHT 90cm (3ft)
SPREAD 90cm (3ft)
SITE Bright light
SOIL John Innes No. 2
HARDINESS Fully hardy
FLOWERING Early summer

O *Oreocereus trollii*

THE ATTRACTIVE OREOCEREUS CACTI, which come from the Andes, have a protective covering of wool and hair-like spines to protect them from the fierce extremes of sun and cold. Some make incredibly tall thin columns, but the pale green *O. trollii* is short and stumpy, branching out from the base and eventually forming a small clump. It has a covering of greyish-white wool, while the spines are yellow, reddish or brown – the small summer flowers are pink to carmine. Bright light is essential; water freely from spring to summer, adding a monthly liquid feed, but keep dry at other times.

OTHER VARIETY *O. aurantiacus* (slightly smaller, with a body made up of wart-like growths; orange-red flowers).

PLANT PROFILE
HEIGHT To 50cm (20in)
SPREAD 25cm (10in)
SITE Full light
SOIL 4 parts standard cactus compost, 1 part limestone chippings
HARDINESS Min 10°C (50°F)
FLOWERING Summer

Pachyphytum oviferum Sugar-almond plant

P

A TINY, CURIOUS, MEXICAN SUCCULENT, the sugar-almond plant consists of spreading clumps of small round growths that are pale blue with an attractive dash of powdery white. The long-lasting dangling flowers are bright orange or greenish-red, and are followed by tiny seed pods. The 60cm (24in) high *P. viride* makes a good companion plant with its slow-growing brown stem (similar to a miniature tree), and rosette of fleshy leaves on top. Provide shade from the hot summer sun and water moderately in the growing season, adding a low-nitrogen liquid feed every six to eight weeks. Keep virtually dry at other times.

OTHER VARIETY *P. compactum* (a more compact succulent with white-frosted dark green leaves and orange-red flowers).

PLANT PROFILE
HEIGHT 15cm (6in)
SPREAD 30cm (12in)
SITE Full light
SOIL Standard cactus compost
HARDINESS Min 7°C (45°F)
FLOWERING Winter to spring

P | *Pachystachys lutea* Lollipop plant

THE 'LOLLIPOPS' REFERRED TO IN THE COMMON NAME are vertical, flashy yellow growths (or bracts – the flowers are actually the white bits), which pop up from the end of spring and continue right through summer. The overall shape is equally impressive, with bushy stems and leaves up to 15cm (6in) long, but an established plant can get bare at the base (if this happens, cut it back in the spring to force up plenty of new growth). It is easy to get *P. lutea* to flower – provide decent humidity, and water freely during the growing season, adding a monthly liquid feed. Water moderately over winter. Look out for whiteflies and red spider mites.

OTHER VARIETY *P. coccinea* (a taller shrub with shorter, scarlet winter flowers).

PLANT PROFILE
HEIGHT To 1m (3ft)
SPREAD To 75cm (30in)
SITE Full light
SOIL John Innes No. 2
HARDINESS Min 13°C (55°F)
FLOWERING Spring and summer

Pandanus veitchii Screw pine

PRIMARILY A FOLIAGE PLANT, the screw pine has long, thin, splendid sword-like leaves that point upwards and outwards. The thin, white stripes make them even more eye-catching, but avoid placing it in too prominent a position (especially with children about) because there are nasty, spiny teeth up the sides of the leaves. High humidity is important for success, as is a light position out of direct, scorching sun, but not in a dark corner. Water moderately from spring to summer, adding a monthly liquid feed; water sparingly in winter. Scale insects and red spider mites may be a problem.

PLANT PROFILE
HEIGHT 1.2m (4ft) or more
SPREAD 1.2m (4ft) or more
SITE Bright light
SOIL John Innes No. 2
HARDINESS Min 13°C (55°F)
FLOWERING Summer

P *Pandorea jasminoides* Bower plant

THIS HIGHLY-RATED AUSTRALIAN EVERGREEN, which climbs way above head height, adds a touch of the rainforest. The glossy, dark green leaves nicely set off the main burst of midsummer flared flowers, which are white with a crimson-pink throat. In warm conditions, it will flower sporadically throughout winter. The stems should be trained up a series of horizontal wires fixed to a conservatory wall. Growth is rarely so rampant as to require pruning (if so, do it after flowering). Water moderately when in full growth, adding a monthly liquid feed; water sparingly in winter. Beware red spider mites and aphids.

OTHER VARIETY *P. jasminoides* 'Lady Di' (white flowers with a typically creamy-yellow throat).

PLANT PROFILE

HEIGHT To 3m (10ft)

SITE Full light

SOIL John Innes No. 3

HARDINESS Min 5°C (41°F)

FLOWERING Spring to summer

Paphiopedilum Goultenianum 'Album' Slipper orchid

P

BEAUTIFULLY COLOURED 'ALBUM' has mottled leaves and superb white spring flowers, with lime green stripes, which last for about two months. Slipper orchids are easy to grow but need to have their roots cramped in pots; also provide high humidity and shade from direct, scorching sun. Water freely over summer, giving it an orchid feed every third watering; water sparingly in winter and always let the soil dry out between drinks. Do not spray with a mister or the drips will fall into the central section and make it rot. Susceptible to red spider mites, aphids and mealybugs.

OTHER VARIETIES *P. bellatulum* (white flowers with red spots), *P. callosum* (maroon and green flowers, with white stripes); *P.* 'Jersey Freckles' (yellow flowers); *P. villosum* (waxy red-brown flowers).

PLANT PROFILE
HEIGHT 30cm (12in)
SPREAD 20cm (8in)
SITE Bright filtered light
SOIL Terrestrial orchid compost
HARDINESS Min 13°C (55°F)
FLOWERING Spring

Parodia mammulosa

P

THE PARODIA CACTI from South America may have an ordinary, small, rounded shape but they become quite special in summer, with incredibly showy flowers. The fast-growing, woolly-crowned *P. mammulosa* bears golden-yellow flowers with a striking dash of red in the middle (the stigmas). About 5cm (2in) wide, the blooms are completely out of proportion to the main body. The white, grey or pale brown spines are short and stiff. Water moderately from mid-spring to late summer, and apply a diluted nitrogen liquid feed every six to eight weeks; keep barely moist at other times. Vulnerable to mealybugs, and aphids when in flower.

OTHER VARIETIES *P. brevihamata* (lemon-yellow flowers, sometimes red tinted); *P. herteri* (pink or purple flowers).

PLANT PROFILE
HEIGHT 10–13cm (4–5in)
SPREAD 6cm (2½in)
SITE Bright filtered light
SOIL Standard cactus compost
HARDINESS Min 10°C (50°F)
FLOWERING Summer

Passiflora quadrangularis Giant granadilla, Passion flower

P

THE PASSION FLOWER (*P. caerulea – see inset*) is often seen growing in gardens, but the giant granadilla is much showier. The large, scented, frilly-edged red flowers – which are 10cm (4in) wide – appear on vigorous every-which-way sprinting stems that can top 15m (50ft) in the wild. Growth is more moderate when restricted in a container but the stems will need to cling to a set of horizontal wall wires. Shade from the hot sun, and replace the top layers of soil in the pot every spring. Water freely in full growth, sparingly over winter. Give a light trim in early spring. Beware red spider mites, whiteflies, mealybugs and scale insects.

OTHER VARIETIES *P. capsularis* (shorter, with small white flowers); *P. morifolia* (white, blue and mauve flowers); *P. vitifolia* (red flowers).

PLANT PROFILE
HEIGHT 3m (10ft)
SITE Full light
SOIL John Innes No. 3
HARDINESS Min 13°C (55°F)
FLOWERING Midsummer to autumn

Pedilanthus tithymaloides 'Variegatus'

SOME PLANTS ARE REASONABLY HAPPY in a dry, centrally-heated atmosphere, one of the largest being *P. tithymaloides*. This succulent, bushy, southern USA/West Indian shrub has zigzagging upright stems, and produces 10cm (4in) long leaves that come in a variety of shapes with pink or white markings. The leaves make an excellent background to the fleshy red 'flowers' (bracts), which have yellow-green at the base. Add sharp sand to the compost to make it more free-draining. Water moderately and apply a monthly liquid feed; water sparingly in winter.

PLANT PROFILE	
HEIGHT	1.2m (4ft)
SPREAD	60cm (24in)
SITE	Bright filtered light
SOIL	John Innes No. 2
HARDINESS	Min 10°C (50°F)
FLOWERING	Summer

Pelargonium 'Apple Blossom Rosebud'

P

AN EXCELLENT, UPRIGHT, BUSHY PELARGONIUM, 'Apple Blossom Rosebud' has a colourful mix of bright green leaves and small pink and white flowers that are locked together in tight clusters up to 8cm (3in) wide. A good choice for a windowsill, it needs to be watered when in full growth, with a liquid feed every 10 to 14 days in spring and early summer. Give it a tomato feed when in flower and water sparingly over winter. Also provide fresh soil each year. Prune hard in late winter to force out plenty of new flowering shoots, and to maintain a compact shape. If the indoor temperature is kept above 7°C (45°F) and there is good light, it may well flower intermittently over winter. Beware aphids.

OTHER VARIETY *P*. 'Plum Rambler' (deep claret flowers).

PLANT PROFILE
HEIGHT 30–40cm (12–16in)
SPREAD 20–25cm (8–10in)
SITE Full sun
SOIL John Innes No. 2
HARDINESS Min 2°C (36°F)
FLOWERING Summer

P

Pelargonium 'Blazonry'

THE LEAVES ARE THE BIG ATTRACTION on 'Blazonry', providing a mix of four colours with cream around the edge, rose-pink and purple zones in the middle, and green right in the centre. This guarantees an eye-catching show even when it is not covered with red flowers. Several plants can either be lined up at the front of a pot plant display, or used as summer bedding for grouping at the front of a bed. To create bushier, leafier plants with only the coloured foliage, keep snipping off the stems that carry the flower buds. 'Blazonry' is usually found listed in catalogues as a 'fancy-leaved zonal pelargonium' or with the variegated kind.

OTHER VARIETY *P.* 'Contrast' (rounded leaves with gold, yellow and red markings, with green in the centre).

PLANT PROFILE

HEIGHT 25–30cm (10–12in)

SPREAD 15–20cm (6–8in)

SITE Full light

SOIL John Innes No. 2

HARDINESS Min 2°C (36°F)

FLOWERING Summer

Pelargonium 'Easter Greeting'

P

CLASSIFIED AS A REGAL PELARGONIUM, 'Easter Greeting' has large, brightly coloured flowers that open relatively early and practically obscure the leaves. The pink petals have a deep, dark wine-red flash in the middle. Regals are slightly fussy and must not be ignored – water regularly with a liquid feed every 10 to 14 days in spring and early summer, and apply a liquid tomato feed when in flower. Water sparingly in winter. It also needs a warmer temperature than the scented-leaved pelargoniums. Prone to aphids.

OTHER VARIETIES *P.* 'Fringed Aztec' (red and white flowers); *P.* 'Georgia Peach' (soft mid-peach and pink flowers), *P.* 'Grand Slam' (crimson-scarlet flowers); *P.* 'Hazel Sager' (rosy-pink flowers, feathered with wine markings); *P.* 'Linda' (orange-red flowers).

PLANT PROFILE	
HEIGHT 25–30cm (10–12in)	
SPREAD 13–18cm (5–7in)	
SITE Full light	
SOIL John Innes No. 2	
HARDINESS Min 7°C (45°F)	
FLOWERING Summer	

P

Pelargonium 'Graveolens'

'GRAVEOLENS' IS AN IMPRESSIVE, BUSHY POT PLANT with plenty of attractive, rich green, divided leaves that have a distinctive smell of tomatoes (although some catalogues say lemons, some roses). The mauve flowers appear in small clusters in summer. There is a wide choice of scented-leaved pelargoniums, all of which can be placed outdoors over summer in a display of pot plants. Shade 'Graveolens' from hot sun and provide ventilation. Water moderately when in full growth, adding a liquid feed every 10 to 14 days in spring and early summer, and provide a liquid tomato feed when in flower; water sparingly in winter. Susceptible to aphids.

OTHER VARIETIES *P. clorinda* (beautiful, with soft pink flowers; gets quite tall and shrubby); *P. tomentosum* (strong peppermint-scented leaves).

PLANT PROFILE
HEIGHT 45–60cm (18–24in)
SPREAD 20–40cm (8–16in)
SITE Full light
SOIL John Innes No. 2
HARDINESS Min 2°C (36°F)
FLOWERING Summer

Pellaea rotundifolia Button fern

P

THIS AUSTRALIAN EVERGREEN FERN gets its common name from the sequence of small, round, leathery leaves that run up each short, poking-out stem. In a small pot, it makes a highly decorative, easily-cared-for houseplant. Ideally, set it against a white background, both for aesthetic reasons, and because it tolerates brighter light than most ferns (but it must remain out of direct sun). It prefers acid (ericaceous) soil, which needs to be kept on the moist side without getting waterlogged. Provide it with a liquid feed every two weeks over summer, and once a month in winter.

PLANT PROFILE

HEIGHT 20cm (8in)

SPREAD 30cm (12in)

SITE Bright filtered light

SOIL Ericaceous

HARDINESS Frost hardy

P *Pentas lanceolata* 'Kermesina' Egyptian star cluster

WITH ITS CLUSTERS OF TINY, STAR-SHAPED, red-throated deep pink flowers, the bushy 'Kermesina' makes a fine show on a windowsill, but it is not that readily available. It can grow quite tall and, if the lower leaves fall off, becomes rather bare at the base but a fairly hard, early spring prune will force out more bushy growth. If kept at about 16°C (60°F) over winter, it will probably carry on flowering, albeit sporadically, out of season. Water freely when in full growth, applying a monthly liquid feed; water sparingly over winter. Beware aphids and red spider mites.

OTHER VARIETIES *P. lanceolata* 'Avalanche' (white variegated leaves with white flowers); *P. lanceolata* 'New Look' (light pink flowers).

PLANT PROFILE
HEIGHT 1.2m (4ft)
SPREAD 1m (3ft)
SITE Bright filtered light
SOIL John Innes No. 2
HARDINESS Min 7°C (45°F)
FLOWERING Summer to autumn

Peperomia caperata 'Luna Red'

P

THERE ARE DIFFERENT FORMS of the excellent *P. caperata*, and 'Luna Red' is certainly the showiest. Its twin attractions are the heart-shaped, dark crimson leaves – which are heavily veined, crinkled and puckered – and the dense show of contrasting, tiny white flowers. Moderate to high humidity is an essential requirement from spring through summer, and in winter it must have full light. Water moderately over the summer, adding a monthly liquid feed; water sparingly in winter, and always use tepid soft water.

OTHER VARIETIES *P. caperata* (heavily-veined, dark green leaves); *P. caperata* 'Tricolor' (creamy margins and pink markings).

PLANT PROFILE

HEIGHT 10cm (4in)

SPREAD 15cm (6in)

SITE Bright indirect light

SOIL John Innes No. 1

HARDINESS Min 15°C (59°F)

FLOWERING Late summer

P

Peperomia glabella Wax privet peperomia

THIS CURIOUS CENTRAL AMERICAN PLANT, which is much more modest than some of the showier peperomias, consists of an upward-pointing cluster of shiny green leaves dotted with black glands. The 8–12cm (3–5in) long spike, which shoots up out of the middle in summer, bears tiny green flowers. Provide moderate to high humidity from spring through summer, and give it full light in winter. Water moderately in summer, adding a monthly liquid feed; give sparing drinks in winter, always using tepid, soft water.

OTHER VARIETY *P. caperata* 'Little Fantasy' (a compact plant, 8cm/3in high, with dark green ornamental leaves).

PLANT PROFILE
HEIGHT 15cm (6in)
SPREAD 30cm (12in)
SITE Bright indirect light
SOIL John Innes No. 1
HARDINESS Min 15°C (59°F)
FLOWERING Late summer

Peperomia obtusifolia 'Variegata' Pepper face

'VARIEGATA', WITH ITS ATTRACTIVELY-PATTERNED glossy leaves that have wide white or yellow margins, makes a far better bet than its non-variegated parent, *P. obtusifolia*. Although growth is small and compact, with white flowers on 9–12cm (3½–5in) long spikes, it is quite bushy and makes an attractive pot plant for the front of a display (*see inset*). Moderate to high humidity is required from spring through summer, and in winter it must have full light. Water moderately in summer, adding a monthly liquid feed; give sparing drinks in winter and always use tepid, soft water.

OTHER VARIETY *P. obtusifolia* 'Green and Gold' (green leaves with golden-yellow margins).

PLANT PROFILE	
HEIGHT 25cm (10in)	
SPREAD 25cm (10in)	
SITE Bright indirect light	
SOIL John Innes No. 1	
HARDINESS Min 15°C (59°F)	
FLOWERING Late summer	

P

Pericallis x *hybrida* 'Brilliant Blue and White' Florists' cineraria

THERE ARE DOZENS OF KINDS of Pericallis, from the compact dwarves (Amigo hybrids) to the taller spreading kind (Moll hybrids). All are good-value plants, being peppered with a cluster of showy, daisy-like flowers that range from white to pink and blue to red. Plants are usually bought in bud and are often discarded after flowering. New plants can be raised from seed sown from spring to summer, at temperatures of 13–18°C (55–64°F). Pericallis hybrids are easy to look after, and must be well watered (without waterlogging) and given good ventilation. Protect against aphids, red spider mites, thrips, whiteflies and chrysanthemum leaf miners.

OTHER VARIETIES There is a wide range of Pericallis hybrids (available in various colours).

PLANT PROFILE

HEIGHT 25cm (10in)

SPREAD 25cm (10in)

SITE Full light

SOIL John Innes No. 2

HARDINESS Min 7°C (45°F)

FLOWERING Winter to spring

Phalaenopsis Lundy Moth orchid

MOTH ORCHIDS WILL GROW all year round, albeit slowly in winter, and in the right conditions flower for about six months. The blooms stay in excellent condition for several weeks but, when a flower drops, cut back the stem to the next bud down from which a new flowering shoot will appear. Grow them in slatted baskets to let the roots poke out; also provide high humidity all year by spraying around the plants, but do not let water drip into the centre because it can cause rotting. Water freely from spring to autumn, and apply a monthly liquid feed; water sparingly in winter, but keep moist. Prone to red spider mites, aphids and mealybugs.

OTHER VARIETIES *P.* Allegria (large, rounded, pure white flowers throughout the year); *P.* Lipperhose (red-lipped pink flowers).

PLANT PROFILE
HEIGHT 60cm (24in)
SITE Bright filtered light
SOIL Epiphytic orchid compost
HARDINESS Min 18°C (64°F); max 30°C (86°F)
FLOWERING Throughout the year

P

Philodendron bipinnatifidum Tree philodendron

TECHNICALLY, THE BRAZILIAN TREE PHILODENDRON is a climber, but
it actually creates a sturdy plant with enormous, lustrous leaves –
about 30cm (12in) long – and stems that arch upwards and outwards
from soil level (*see inset*). When young, the leaves are heart-shaped,
but they gradually divide into sections of about a dozen or more
long fingers, creating a jungly, exotic effect. Give it a regular spray to
create humidity and water freely when in full growth, adding a
monthly liquid feed; water sparingly in winter. Scale insects and red
spider mites may be a problem.

PLANT PROFILE
HEIGHT 2m (6ft)
SPREAD 60cm (24in)
SITE Bright filtered or indirect light
SOIL Loamless compost
HARDINESS Min 15°C (59°F)
FLOWERING Occasionally

Philodendron melanochrysm Black gold philodendron

P

ONE OF THE BEST CLIMBING FOLIAGE PLANTS for a conservatory, black gold philodendron has heart-shaped leaves that are typically 25cm (10in) long, but in ideal conditions they can grow even longer. Young plants have smaller, broader, copper-red leaves, but when established they are quite superb; they have a velvety sheen on the blackish-green surface, and beautiful, pale green veins. The rare, insignificant flowers are best removed. Grow it up a moss pole and spray regularly to create humidity. Water freely when in full growth and add a monthly liquid feed; water sparingly in winter. Susceptible to scale insects and red spider mites.

OTHER VARIETY *P. erubescens* (the blushing philodendron has glossy, arrow-shaped leaves that reach 1.8m/6ft or more).

PLANT PROFILE
HEIGHT 2m (8ft)
SPREAD 1m (3ft)
SITE Bright filtered or indirect light
SOIL Loamless compost
HARDINESS Min 15°C (59°F)
FLOWERING Occasionally

P

Phoenix roebelenii Miniature date palm

THE SLOW-GROWING MINIATURE DATE PALM initially throws out long, soft, arching leaves divided into thin strips or fingers, creating an open, elegant look. At this point, it is a first-rate palm, but it will not really start growing tall until it has developed a thick sturdy trunk, which takes a few years (*see inset*). Shade it from hot sun, and spray to create some humidity. Replace the top layer of soil each spring – this is better than tipping the plant out of the pot because it hates root disturbance. Water freely when in full growth and apply a monthly liquid feed; water sparingly in winter. Beware scale insects and red spider mites.

OTHER VARIETY *P. canariensis* (it grows much bigger – after eight years it will need to be discarded).

PLANT PROFILE
HEIGHT 2m (6ft)
SPREAD 90cm (3ft)
SITE Full light
SOIL John Innes No. 2
HARDINESS Min 10–16°C (50–61°F)

Phormium 'Sundowner'

PHORMIUMS MAKE SUPERB ARCHITECTURAL PLANTS with a great upward-shooting mass of strap-like leaves. On 'Sundowner', they are an attractive bronze-green, with pink margins. Stand the pots outside over summer or plant in the border, but bring indoors over winter to escape cold, wet soil and icy winds. Water well over summer, adding a liquid feed every two weeks; keep just moist in winter. Mature plants may need dividing every few years in the spring to constrain growth. To do this, insert two forks, back to back, into the clump and gently prise apart. Replant a small portion with good roots.

OTHER VARIETY *P.* 'Dazzler' (slightly smaller with bronze leaves striped red, orange, and pink).

PLANT PROFILE
HEIGHT 1.2m (4ft)
SPREAD 1.2m (4ft)
SITE Full sun
SOIL John Innes No. 2
HARDINESS Frost hardy
FLOWERING Summer

P

Pilea cadierei

THIS HIGHLY-RATED SMALL FOLIAGE PLANT has beautiful, textured, tactile leaves – they are dark green with four raised silver patches and grow in distinctive pairs (one always opposite the other). It may lose leaves lower down while being quite bushy higher up – the best solution is to nip out the growing tips in the spring, which will also create a pleasing, mounded shape (*see inset*). Provide bright light and moderate to high humidity. Water moderately during the growing season, adding a monthly liquid feed, and allow the surface to dry out between watering; give a sparing drink in winter. Protect against powdery mildew.

OTHER VARIETY *P. involucrata* 'Norfolk' (the bronze leaves have prominent, raised areas coloured silver).

PLANT PROFILE

HEIGHT 30cm (12in)

SPREAD 16–21cm (6–8in)

SITE Bright indirect light

SOIL Loamless compost

HARDINESS Min 15°C (59°F)

Pilea depressa

P

AN UNOBTRUSIVE, COLOURFUL PLANT, *P. depressa* is ideal for a small space on a windowsill or shelf. The thin stems, which initially poke up and then trail over the sides of the pot, are covered with fleshy, bright green leaves (*see inset*). It can also be grown in a hanging basket as a filler because it is not dramatic enough to be the star plant. Provide bright light and moderate to high humidity. Water moderately during the growing season, adding a monthly liquid feed, and allow the surface to dry out between watering; water sparingly in winter. Prone to powdery mildew.

OTHER VARIETY *P. nummulariifolia* (creeping Charlie is good in hanging baskets because of its trailing growth and light green leaves).

PLANT PROFILE
HEIGHT 10cm (4in)
SPREAD 30cm (12in)
SITE Bright indirect light
SOIL Loamless compost
HARDINESS Min 15°C (59°F)

P | *Pilea involucrata* Friendship plant

A FIRST-RATE, EYE-CATCHING PILEA, it has extraordinary, tactile leaves that are dark green in the centre, with a pale green band running right round the outside. The thickly-textured leaves, made up of tiny segments, are beautifully arranged in pairs. Growth is very vigorous and creates a bushy, mounded effect (*see inset*). Provide bright light and moderate to high humidity. Water moderately during the growing season, adding a monthly liquid feed, and allow the surface to dry out between watering; give a sparing drink in winter. Powdery mildew may be a problem.

OTHER VARIETY *P. involucrata* 'Moon Valley' (more upright and open, with fresh green leaves with sunken purple veins).

PLANT PROFILE

HEIGHT 3cm (1¼in)

SPREAD 25cm (10in)

SITE Bright indirect light

SOIL Loamless compost

HARDINESS Min 15°C (59°F)

Pilea microphylla Artillery plant

THE ARTILLERY PLANT IS FUN FOR CHILDREN because when it is given a shake the pollen that covers its tiny, insignificant summer flowers flies up like smoke, as if a battery of guns has been fired. The crowded, small mossy leaves, which are bright green and appear on thick, fleshy erect stems, give it plenty of packed growth (*see inset*). Provide bright light and moderate to high humidity. Water moderately during the growing season, adding a monthly liquid feed, and allow the surface to dry out between watering; water sparingly in winter. Susceptible to powdery mildew.

PLANT PROFILE	
HEIGHT 30cm (12in)	
SPREAD 30cm (12in)	
SITE Bright indirect light	
SOIL Loamless compost	
HARDINESS Min 15°C (59°F)	
FLOWERING Summer	

P

Piper longum Pepper

THIS RARE, SLENDER-STEMMED CLIMBER has oval pointy leaves and, coming from the tropical eastern Himalayas, needs a humid atmosphere. It belongs to the same family as the woody-stemmed *P. nigrum*, which provides commercial peppercorns. A good alternative is *P. ornatum* (*see inset*), which has olive green, with a dash of silvery-pink, heart-shaped leaves. It can be grown either as a trailing plant with stems dangling over the pot, or as a climber with its stems tied to a moss pole. It too needs good humidity, and both pipers require fast-draining soil with sharp sand added to the compost. Water moderately over summer but sparingly in winter. Avoid sudden changes in temperature and draughts. Prune in late winter to curtail its spread if necessary.

PLANT PROFILE
HEIGHT 3m (9ft)
SITE Full light
SOIL John Innes No. 3
HARDINESS Min. 16°C (60°F)
FLOWERING Summer

Platycerium bifurcatum Common staghorn fern

P

THE BIZARRE COMMON STAGHORN FERN has two kinds of leaves.
The heart-shaped ones grab hold of the tree they are climbing up,
and act as a kind of dustbin for any debris falling down from high
above (which then rots down and gets absorbed by the plant). The
other grey-green leaves, which poke out or down, grow up to
90cm (3ft) long in the wild and resemble antlers. It is best grown
by wrapping the roots in sphagnum moss and tying it with fishing
line to a length of wood (*see inset*), although it can also be grown in
a pot. Water freely when in full growth, applying a monthly liquid
feed, and mist daily to create some humidity. Water sparingly in
winter. Vulnerable to scale insects.

PLANT PROFILE

HEIGHT 90cm (3ft)

SPREAD 80cm (32in)

SITE Bright filtered light

SOIL Equal parts leafmould
or peat substitute,
sphagnum moss and
charcoal

HARDINESS Min 5°C
(41°F)

P

Plectranthus amboinicus

THIS MODEST LITTLE SOUTH AFRICAN PLANT is best grown in a hanging basket, ideally as a filler and not as the main feature. The none-too-vigorous spreading growth has hairy, scented leaves dotted with tiny glands; the edges are finely scalloped. In summer, the clusters of small, two-lipped flowers give a gentle display of lilac-pink, mauve or white. Provide some shade from potentially scorching, hot summer sun. Water freely when in full growth, adding a monthly liquid feed; water moderately over winter. *P. amboinicus* seems quite happy in the dry atmosphere of a room with central heating.

OTHER VARIETY *P. oertendahlii* (trailing stems with rounded leaves and silver veins; leaves are green above and purple beneath).

PLANT PROFILE

HEIGHT	23cm (9in)
SPREAD	60cm (24in)
SITE	Full light
SOIL	John Innes No. 2
HARDINESS	Min 10°C (50°F)
FLOWERING	Summer

Pleione formosana

P

ONE OF THE EASIEST ORCHIDS to look after, the pale rose-lilac flower of *P. formosana* has white lips with dark spots, pink margins and brownish markings. Though small, the flower is quite special and lasts for about ten days. Because each plant has only a single bloom, grow several in one shallow container for a decent display. Plant the bulbs with the top half protruding above the surface, and do not water until the flower buds appear. Water well in spring and summer; add a liquid feed every third watering until the leaves die down, and then keep just moist. Repot annually while dormant, before flowering. Beware aphids, red spider mites and mealybugs.

OTHER VARIETY *P. humilis* (smaller white flowers in winter, sometimes with a scattering of purple spots).

PLANT PROFILE
HEIGHT 15cm (6in)
SPREAD 15cm (6in)
SITE Bright filtered light
SOIL Epiphytic orchid compost
HARDINESS Half hardy
FLOWERING Spring

P

Plumbago auriculata Cape leadwort

ONE OF THE MOST STRIKING CONSERVATORY PLANTS, with showy heads of sky blue flowers, Cape leadwort is a straggly climber and needs horizontal wires to thread through. Plant it in a border or, with limited space, restrict it to 90cm (3ft) high, growing it around a wire loop in a 23cm (9in) pot, and stand it outside in summer (*see inset*). Either way, prune in early spring and/or winter, leaving one-third of the length of last year's flowering stems. Provide shade from scorching sun and water freely during the growing season, giving a monthly liquid feed; water sparingly in winter. Red spider mites, whiteflies and mealybugs may be a problem.

OTHER VARIETY *P. auriculata* var. *alba* (pure white flowers).

PLANT PROFILE

HEIGHT To 2.4m (8ft)

SPREAD To 1.2m (4ft)

SITE Full light

SOIL John Innes No. 3

HARDINESS Min 4°C (40°F)

FLOWERING Summer to autumn

Plumeria rubra Common frangipani

THIS IMPOSING, CENTRAL AMERICAN SHRUBBY PLANT has a tall branching shape and thick stems that produce attractive long leaves, often with a red tinge. Clusters of yellow-eyed, rose-pink flowers (sometimes yellow or red to bronze) appear over summer. Its size demands a place in the conservatory border, or in a large pot, where it is very easy to look after. Provide shade from direct, hot summer sun, and water moderately when in full growth, adding a monthly liquid feed. Keep virtually dry (never bone dry) when it is dormant over winter. Protect against red spider mites. Prune for size in late winter, but wear gloves because the sap is toxic.

OTHER VARIETY *P. rubra* var. *acutifolia* (dark green leaves; highly scented, yellow-eyed white flowers from late summer to autumn).

PLANT PROFILE
HEIGHT 2.5m (8ft)
SPREAD 2m (6ft)
SITE Full light
SOIL John Innes No. 2
HARDINESS Min 10–13°C (50–55°F)
FLOWERING Summer to autumn

P

Polyscias filicifolia Fern-leaf aralia

AN ERECT EVERGREEN SHRUB capable of exceeding 2.5m (8ft) high in the Pacific region, fern-leaf aralia has a mass of beautifully divided bright green leaves and purplish stems. It can be tricky to grow but is certainly not impossible. Nip out the tips of young plants to make them branch more, but note that it will take a while for significant results because it is slow growing in the early stages. Provide decent humidity, maintain a constant temperature and keep it out of any draughts. Water freely when in full growth, applying a monthly liquid feed; water sparingly in winter. Prone to red spider mites and mealybugs.

OTHER VARIETY *P. guilfoylei* (the coffee tree is a large evergreen shrub with large leaves but few branches).

PLANT PROFILE
HEIGHT 1.2m (4ft)
SPREAD 1m (3ft)
SITE Bright filtered light
SOIL John Innes No. 3
HARDINESS Min 16°C (61°F)

Primula obconica 'Cantata Lavender' Primrose

THE OBCONICA PRIMROSES give a lovely winter to spring show, with heads of large flat flowers – those of 'Cantata Lavender' are lavender-blue. All are best grown as annuals because the first display is the best, after which the plants are best discarded. Water freely when in full growth, applying a half-strength liquid feed every week. Plants are best handled when wearing gloves because the chemicals on the hairs can give a nasty allergic reaction. Beware red spider mites and aphids.

OTHER VARIETY *P. obconica* 'Appleblossom' (large pale pink flowers that turn salmon-pink, and then reddish-pink); *P. obconica* 'Pin Up' (free-flowering, with rose-pink flowers); *P. obconica* 'Queen of the Market' (reddish-pink flowers).

PLANT PROFILE
HEIGHT 23–40cm (9–16in)
SPREAD To 25cm (10in)
SITE Bright filtered light
SOIL 4 parts John Innes No. 2, 1 part grit, 1 part leafmould
HARDINESS Frost hardy
FLOWERING Winter and spring

P | *Prostanthera rotundifolia* Round–leaved mint bush

THIS EXCEPTIONAL AUSTRALIAN SHRUB has very thin stems and spreading growth with small, deep green, mint-scented leaves, which give an airy, elegant look. In late spring, there is an abundant show of bell-shaped purple-to-lilac flowers, which adds a refreshing touch and makes it one of the best conservatory plants at this time of year. It can easily be grown in a pot or conservatory border, but deserves a prominent position. Cut back the flowered shoots to within 2.5cm (1in) of the old growth after flowering. Water moderately when in growth, applying a monthly liquid feed; water sparingly in winter. Susceptible to red spider mites and whiteflies.

OTHER VARIETIES *P. cuneata* (half as high, with white summer flowers); *P. melissifolia* (with a slightly stronger scent).

PLANT PROFILE

HEIGHT 2m (6ft)

SPREAD 1m (3ft)

SITE Full light

SOIL John Innes No. 2

HARDINESS Half hardy

FLOWERING Late spring and early summer

Psychopsis papilio Butterfly orchid

A SPECTACULAR CENTRAL AND SOUTH AMERICAN ORCHID, *P. papilio* has two-winged, orange-brown flowers with three long 'antennae' poking out. Hard to miss, the blooms appear on stems up to 1.2m (4ft) high that should be left in case more flowers appear. The easiest way to grow it is in a conservatory pot, but it needs high summer temperatures, from 30°C (85°C), with high humidity, and an occasional drink of rainwater with a liquid feed. Maintain the high humidity throughout winter, and keep at a minimum of 18.5°C (65°F), but water less because it is dormant. It prefers being cramped in a pot and not moved into a larger container.

OTHER VARIETY *P. krameriana* (the large, spotted yellow flowers last for two weeks).

PLANT PROFILE

HEIGHT 1.2m (4ft)

SPREAD 30cm (12in)

SITE Full light

SOIL Epiphytic orchid compost

HARDINESS Min 10°C (50°F)

FLOWERING Any time throughout the year

P

Pteris argyraea Silver brake

A TROPICAL, BRIGHTLY COLOURED FERN, silver brake has large, 30in (75cm) long, leaves – divided into pairs of mini-leaflets – with silvery-white stripes down the centre. Coming from tropical climates, it should have high humidity, and can be placed in a pot or planted in a border that is well out of direct, scorching sun. Water freely when it is in full growth, applying a monthly, high-nitrogen liquid feed (which promotes good leaf growth); water much more sparingly in winter. Beware scale insects.

OTHER VARIETY *P. biaurita* (without the white variegation).

PLANT PROFILE
HEIGHT 75cm (30in)
SPREAD 75cm (30in)
SITE Bright filtered light
SOIL 1 part sharp sand, leafmould and charcoal, 2 parts John Innes No. 2 with limestone chips
HARDINESS Min 10°C (50°F)

Pteris cretica var. *albolineata*

P

THIS EVERGREEN FERN from Europe, Africa and Asia has an abundant mass of crowded, arching fronds and makes a buoyant, eye-catching background filler (*see inset*). There are several attractive forms of *P. cretica*, some more vigorous and others more compact. This variegated kind is very easy to grow, but does need high humidity and a place that is out of direct, scorching sun. Water freely when it is in full growth, applying a monthly, high-nitrogen liquid feed; water much more sparingly in winter. Scale insects may be a problem.

OTHER VARIETIES *P. cretica* 'Parkeri' (vigorous and bigger); *P. cretica* 'Wimsetti' (more compact, but no variegation).

PLANT PROFILE
HEIGHT 45cm (18in)
SPREAD 45cm (18in)
SITE Bright filtered light
SOIL 1 part sharp sand, leafmould and charcoal, 2 parts John Innes No. 2 with limestone chips
HARDINESS Min 2°C (36°F)

Punica granatum var. *nana* Pomegranate

P

THIS COMPACT, SPINY SHRUB, found growing from central Europe to the Himalayas, has three good attractions – the glossy, bright green leaves which, when young, have copper or red veins; the long, quirky, bright orange-red flowers; and the yellow-brown round fruit. Its size demands a large pot or a place in a border where it can be clearly seen and will not be crowded by other plants, not least because it needs plenty of light. Water freely when in full growth, applying a monthly liquid feed; water sparingly in winter. It must have 13–16°C (55–61°F) in the autumn to help the fruit ripen.

OTHER VARIETY *P. granatum* (over twice as high, does not fruit as abundantly).

PLANT PROFILE
HEIGHT 75cm (30in)
SPREAD 75cm (30in)
SITE Full light
SOIL John Innes No. 2
HARDINESS Frost hardy
FLOWERING Summer

Puya mirabilis

P

A SOUTH AMERICAN PLANT (found in Bolivia and Argentina, where it is pollinated by humming birds), *P. mirabilis* has an attractive wide-spreading rosette of leaves that hugs the ground. The white to brownish-green leaves, which are edged with tiny 'teeth', are initially upright but become more horizontal as they develop. The yellow-green summer flowers appear in clusters and are quite beautiful when seen close-up. Water only moderately from mid-spring through to the end of summer, and apply a half-strength nitrogen liquid feed every six to eight weeks. At other times, water more sparingly, but note that it will not tolerate standing in potentially lethal, cold wet soil over winter.

PLANT PROFILE
HEIGHT 10cm (4in)
SPREAD 60cm (24in)
SITE Full light
SOIL Terrestrial bromeliad compost
HARDINESS Min 5°C (41°F)
FLOWERING Summer

P | *Pyrostegia venusta* Golden shower

A MAGNIFICENT, EVERGREEN, South American jungle vine, golden shower bears superb bunches of bright reddish-orange flowers in winter. It can easily climb 10m (30ft) high in the wild, but only reaches about half that in a conservatory where it needs to be grown in a border with some support for its tendrils (which shoot out from between the leaf pairs). Train the growth up a wall, and then along the roof so that the flowers can dangle down. After flowering, either give it a light prune or shorten the side-shoots – leaving three to four buds – to keep it in check. Water moderately during the growing season, adding a monthly liquid feed; water sparingly in winter. Scale insects and red spider mites may be a problem.

PLANT PROFILE

HEIGHT 4.5m (13½ft)

SITE Full light

SOIL John Innes No. 2

HARDINESS Min 10–13°C (50–55°F)

FLOWERING Winter

Ravenea rivularis Majesty palm

THE EXTREMELY ELEGANT, fast-growing majesty palm, from
Madagascar, has upward-arching leaves that are divided into long,
thin fingers. It makes a fine conservatory feature plant, but make
sure that there is a high roof because, in the right conditions, it can
get quite tall (*see inset*). Relatively easy to grow, it tolerates low light
and cool conditions but needs decent summer humidity – a dry
atmosphere can be fatal. Water well over summer, but only when
the soil surface dries (to avoid waterlogging), and add a liquid feed
every two weeks; keep just moist in winter.

R

PLANT PROFILE
HEIGHT 3m (10ft) or more
SPREAD 1.5m (5ft) or more
SITE Bright filtered light
SOIL John Innes No. 3
HARDINESS Min 10°C (50°F)

R | *Rehmannia elata* Chinese foxglove

THE DELIGHTFUL, SMALL, FOXGLOVE-LIKE FLOWERS of *R. elata* appear on short, wiry stems, producing a bright show of purple-pink with a flash of yellow throat. It can be placed outside in a pot plant display or grown in sheltered borders with rich, free-draining soil, but must be brought back inside over winter to avoid the cold and wet. Water freely when in growth, applying a monthly liquid feed; keep just moist in winter. Alternatively, grow fresh plants from seed each year, sowing it at 13–16°C (55–61°F) in multi-purpose compost in late winter for flowering in about 12 month's time. Prone to slugs and snails.

OTHER VARIETY *R. glutinosa* (a perennial – half as high, with yellow-brown lipped flowers and brownish throats).

PLANT PROFILE
HEIGHT 75cm (30in)
SPREAD 60cm (24in)
SITE Bright filtered light
SOIL John Innes No. 2
HARDINESS Fully hardy
FLOWERING Summer to autumn

Rhapis excelsa Miniature fan palm

R

THE STRIKINGLY ARCHITECTURAL MINIATURE FAN PALM, originally from China, is well worth growing for its dark green, fan-like leaves, which are about 20cm (8in) long and have up to ten fingers (*see inset*). It is slow growing – which means mature plants are very expensive to buy – and will only need potting up to a larger container every couple of years. If it ever does get too big to keep, plant it outside for one final summer (it will die in the winter cold) and then buy a younger plant for the conservatory. Mist regularly to stop the leaf tips turning brown and water freely over summer, giving a monthly liquid feed; water moderately in winter. Protect against red spider mites.

PLANT PROFILE
HEIGHT 1.2m (4ft)
SPREAD 1.2m (4ft)
SITE Bright filtered light
SOIL Loamless potting compost
HARDINESS Min 10–13°C (50-55°F)
FLOWERING Summer

R

Rhipsalis cereuscula

OFTEN CALLED THE CORAL CACTUS, the fern-like, South American *R. cereuscula* puts out a thick mass of trailing stems, making it a very good choice for a hanging basket. Each stem develops several short shoots at the end, which, in turn, sometimes produce aerial roots. The funnel-shaped, white flowers appear in the spring (*see inset*) and are followed by berry-like, round white fruit. It is easy to grow – just provide moderate to high humidity and keep it out of direct sun (rhipsalis are shade-loving plants from wooded and forested areas). Water freely when in full growth, adding a liquid feed on three to four occasions; water sparingly at other times.

OTHER VARIETY *R. teres* (fast growing with thick, stiff stems, fern-like leaves and white to greenish-white flowers).

PLANT PROFILE

HEIGHT 60cm (24in)

SPREAD 40cm (16in)

SITE Bright filtered light

SOIL Epiphytic cactus compost

HARDINESS Min 7–12°C (45–54°F)

FLOWERING Spring

Rhododendron 'Inga' Indian azalea

R

ONE OF THE MANY EXCELLENT winter-flowering azaleas (originally from China, not India) that are widely available over Christmas, 'Inga' has dark pink flowers with a pale pink border set against the dark green leaves (*see inset*). It is unfussy with temperatures, and withstands a cool winter conservatory, but note that it should not be planted outside now because the frost will kill it. Provide moderate to high humidity, and keep moist using rainwater (but do not get it waterlogged); use an ericaceous liquid feed every two weeks. Repot after flowering and plant it outside over summer in a shady, moist position; pot up and bring it indoors at the end of summer.

OTHER VARIETIES *R.* 'Ambrosia' (cherry red flowers); *R.* 'Hexe' (trusses of rich crimson flowers).

PLANT PROFILE
HEIGHT 40cm (16in)
SPREAD 50cm (20in)
SITE Bright to moderate
SOIL Ericaceous
HARDINESS Min 3–7°C (38–45°F)
FLOWERING Winter

R *Rhoicissus capensis* Cape grape

THIS VERY POPULAR, COMPLETELY UNFUSSY CLIMBER is easily grown up supporting canes in a pot. The stems produce a good covering of leathery, shiny, round to kidney-shaped dark green leaves that make an excellent background for brightly coloured houseplants. The ultimate size of the plant depends on the size of the pot. If it is kept restricted in a small container and gently pruned in the spring, it may never exceed 90cm (3ft). If you want it to reach 4.5m (15ft) or more, it will need plenty of root space in a conservatory border. Water moderately when in full growth and apply a monthly liquid feed; water sparingly in winter.

PLANT PROFILE

HEIGHT 2m (6ft)

SPREAD 60cm (24in)

SITE Full light

SOIL John Innes No. 2

HARDINESS Min 7°C (45°F)

Ruellia devosiana

R

A SMALL, HAIRY BRAZILIAN SHRUB, *R. devosiana* has superb, soft leaves and beautiful flowers. The leaves, a bit like elongated triangles, grow up to 8cm (3in) long and have highly distinctive pale green veins set against the dark green background. This helps set off the small, funnel-shaped, white flowers that are gently tinged lavender-blue. Prune the young shoots in spring to induce extra bushy growth. Provide high humidity levels and water freely when in full growth, applying a monthly liquid feed; water moderately over winter.

OTHER VARIETY *R. makoyana* (the monkey plant is a slightly larger trailing plant, 45cm/18in wide, with rich pink summer flowers).

PLANT PROFILE
HEIGHT 45cm (18in)
SPREAD 30cm (12in)
SITE Bright filtered light
SOIL Loamless potting compost
HARDINESS Min 12°C (54°F)
FLOWERING Spring to summer

S

Sabal minor Dwarf palmetto

THE NORTH AMERICAN DWARF PALMETTO has fan-shaped blue-green leaves that are nicely divided into slender fingers, giving it a lush, luxuriant look. Keep it at around 1.2m (4ft) high by growing it in a 30cm (12in) pot and restricting its root growth – this also allows it to be transferred outside over summer into a scheme for architectural, jungly plants. Alternatively, grow it in a conservatory border. You will need a male and a female plant for it to flower, although it is unlikely to bloom in a conservatory. Provide some humidity, and also fresh compost for pots each spring. Water moderately through the growing season, applying a monthly liquid feed; keep just moist in winter.

PLANT PROFILE

HEIGHT 2m (6ft)

SPREAD 2m (6ft)

SITE Bright indirect light

SOIL John Innes No. 2

HARDINESS Min 5–7°C (41–45°F)

FLOWERING Rarely

Saintpaulia 'Kristi Marie' African violet

S

THERE ARE MANY good-value African violets in a wide range of flower colours, including the dusky red of 'Kristi Marie'. They can be grown as houseplants or in a conservatory, but are slightly tricky to keep. For year-long intermittent flowers (which will appear above the rosette of hairy leaves), provide decent humidity, put the plants in bright light (out of direct, scorching sun) in summer, and give them the brightest winter light available. From early to late summer, water moderately, applying a one-quarter strength liquid feed with every watering – water from beneath (to avoid splashing and marking the leaves) by filling the saucer; water sparingly in winter.

OTHER VARIETIES *S.* 'Dorothy' (pink with frilled white margins); *S.* 'King's Treasure' (lavender flowers); *S.* 'Tomahawk' (dark red flowers).

PLANT PROFILE
HEIGHT 15–20cm (6–8in)
SPREAD 20–40cm (8–16in)
SITE Bright filtered light
SOIL Loamless compost
HARDINESS Min 15°C (59°F)
FLOWERING Intermittently all year

S

Sanchezia speciosa

A CHUNKY, SOUTH AMERICAN EVERGREEN SHRUB for the conservatory border, *S. speciosa* only makes average bushy growth with sturdy stems. It compensates by having glossy, dark green leaves, about 15cm (6in) long, which are brightly marked with yellow, ivory or white veins. The best show comes in summer, with clusters of six to ten showy yellow flowers, parts of which are red. If necessary, give it a light prune after flowering to maintain a pleasing, regular shape. Provide shade from hot sun, and water freely when in full growth; water sparingly in winter. Beware red spider mites and scale insects.

PLANT PROFILE	
HEIGHT 1.2m (4ft)	
SPREAD 90cm (3ft)	
SITE Full light	
SOIL John Innes No. 2	
HARDINESS Min 13–15°C (55–59°F)	
FLOWERING Summer	

Sandersonia aurantiaca

S

A SHORT, AFRICAN CLIMBER, *S. aurantiaca* is actually a bulb-like perennial that barely reaches more than thigh high. It attracts plenty of attention for its strange and striking bright orange flowers that resemble little urns on thin, weak stems. It will need some kind of support, otherwise the stems tend to flop over, masking the flowers. Water freely when in full growth, giving a monthly liquid feed; reduce the watering as the leaves fade, and keep dry while dormant in winter. *S. aurantiaca* is rarely referred to in gardening books, but it is available from specialist bulb suppliers and nurseries.

PLANT PROFILE

HEIGHT 75cm (30in)

SPREAD 10cm (4in)

SITE Full light

SOIL 4 parts John Innes No. 2 to 1 part grit

HARDINESS Half hardy

FLOWERING Summer

S

Sansevieria trifasciata 'Golden Hahnii' **Mother–in–law's tongue**

UNLIKE THE TYPICAL MOTHER–IN–LAW'S TONGUE, which can easily exceed 60cm (24in) in height with its stiff, vertical leaves, this is a miniature version that grows in a completely different way. The low-growing leaves, which make a very attractive, ground-hugging rosette, are golden-yellow with a broad, green stripe running up the centre. Only move it into the next-sized pot when the roots are well packed inside the current container. Water moderately when in full growth, applying a monthly, half-strength liquid feed; water sparingly in winter.

OTHER VARIETY *S. trifasciata* 'Laurentii' (the well-known mother-in-law's tongue grows up to 1.2m/4ft tall, with yellow-striped leaves – *see inset*).

PLANT PROFILE
HEIGHT 12cm (5in)
SPREAD 12cm (5in)
SITE Bright filtered light
SOIL John Innes No. 2
HARDINESS Min 13°C (55°F)

Sarracenia x *catesbyi* Pitcher plant

S

THE HIGHLY EFFECTIVE, CARNIVOROUS pitcher plant is not snappy like the Venus fly trap, but does make a very effective edge-of-pond plant, inside or out. Insects are attracted largely by the nectar – they tumble down to the bottom or work their way in until they find no foothold – and end up being digested by the plant's enzymes. Pitchers tend to be either green, yellow–green or red, often with attractive patterning or veins. To water, stand the bottom of the pots in rainwater (not tap water). Leave them outside in sheltered areas over winter or bring indoors – they should flower the following spring before the new pitchers start shooting up.

OTHER VARIETY *S. flava* (yellow trumpet is one of the easiest pitchers to grow; golden green with red marks in the throat and hood).

PLANT PROFILE	
HEIGHT To 30cm (12in)	
SPREAD To 30cm (12in)	
SITE Bright light	
SOIL John Innes No. 2	
HARDINESS Frost hardy	
FLOWERING Summer	

Saxifraga stolonifera 'Tricolor' Mother of thousands

THE BEST WAY TO GROW mother of thousands is in a hanging basket so that the long thin 'cords', with the new young plants growing on the ends, dangle over the sides (*see inset*). If snipped off in spring or early summer, the babies can then be planted in pots of multi-purpose compost where they will take root and create extra plants. The green leaves, patterned with red and white marks, are an extra bonus. In summer, it bears tiny, white flowers with yellow or red spots. Keep out of direct, scorching sun and water well when in full growth, adding a monthly liquid feed and keeping the compost moist; water sparingly over winter.

PLANT PROFILE

HEIGHT To 30cm (12in)

SPREAD To 30cm (12in)

SITE Bright light

SOIL John Innes No. 2

HARDINESS Frost hardy

FLOWERING Summer

Scadoxus multiflorus subsp. *katherinae* Blood lily

S

THIS SPECTACULAR, ALMOST EVERGREEN, tropical, South African plant produces a tall stem, topped by a large ball consisting of scores of tiny red flowers followed by small orange berries. The leaves, which can be up to 23cm (9in) long, have a wavy edge and form a cluster at the base of the stem. Despite looking exotically showy, it is easy to grow. Provide shade from hot sun, and move into partial shade as the buds start opening. Water freely when in full growth, and apply a monthly, half-strength liquid feed. As the leaves begin to fade, reduce watering and give just the occasional drink over winter when dormant. Provide fresh soil each spring.

OTHER VARIETY *S. multiflorus* (a slightly shorter plant, without the wavy edges on the leaves).

PLANT PROFILE
HEIGHT 90cm (3ft)
SPREAD 60cm (24in)
SITE Full light
SOIL John Innes No. 2
HARDINESS Min 10–15°C (50–59°F)
FLOWERING Summer

S | *Schefflera elegantissima* False aralia

FALSE ARALIA WILL GROW up to a height of about 3m (10ft), but to keep it fairly short – about 90cm (3ft) high – place it in a small pot; the larger the container, the more it will shoot up. The young leaves are a big attraction; shaped like long, thin, splayed-open fingers, they are dark green but look black from a distance (*see inset*). Keep plants at a constant temperature and out of draughts, and only water moderately when in growth, applying a monthly liquid feed; keep just moist in winter. Protect against scale insects, thrips and mealybugs.

OTHER VARIETY *S. arboricola* 'Trinetta' (an upright plant for growing up a moss pole, with bright yellow markings on the leaves).

PLANT PROFILE

HEIGHT To 2m (6ft)

SPREAD 90cm (3ft)

SITE Bright filtered light

SOIL John Innes No. 2

HARDINESS Min 13–15°C (55–59°F)

Schizanthus pinnatus 'Hit Parade' Poor man's orchid

S

THE FLOWERS OF THIS BRIGHT, FLASHY, EXUBERANT ANNUAL have a lipstick-pink flared mouth and yellow throat with dark marks. It can be bought in the spring from garden centres, or you can sow seed in mid-spring, at 16°C (61°F), in multi purpose compost for a flowering period running from summer to autumn – or sow seed in late summer for a show of winter flowers. Nip out the tips of young plants to create more flowering stems. After flowering, the plants can be discarded. Provide shade from direct, hot sun, and water moderately when in full growth, applying a tomato liquid feed every two weeks. Aphids may be a problem.

OTHER VARIETY *S. pinnatus* 'Star Parade' (more compact form, reaching 25cm/10in).

PLANT PROFILE
HEIGHT 23–30cm (9–12in)
SPREAD 23–30cm (9–12in)
SITE Bright filtered light
SOIL John Innes No. 2
HARDINESS Min 5°C (41°F)
FLOWERING Spring to autumn

S

Schlumbergera truncata Crab cactus

THERE IS A WIDE RANGE of safe-to-handle, spineless Christmas cactuses, each with a packed cluster of flattened, green stems that arch out over the pot's rim, bearing bright, brash flowers right at the tips. The crab cactus tends to start off like a small bush but gradually becomes much more prostrate – the flowers are bright red, orange, deep pink or white. Provide average humidity and water moderately, applying a monthly liquid tomato feed when in full growth; water sparingly after flowering. Stand outside in the summer in a sheltered, shady part of the garden and water more regularly once it starts growing again. Prone to mealybugs.

OTHER VARIETIES *S.* 'Bristol Beauty' (a good show of reddish-purple flowers); *S.* 'Spectabile Coccineum' (bright red flowers).

PLANT PROFILE

HEIGHT To 30cm (12in)

SPREAD 30cm (12in)

SITE Bright indirect light

SOIL Epiphytic cactus compost

HARDINESS Min 10°C (50°F)

FLOWERING Winter

Scindapsus pictus argyraeum

S

THIS EASILY-GROWN HOUSEPLANT can shoot up to 2m (6ft) high if it is grown against a wall. In a pot, it just needs a moss-covered pole to climb around, which is an excellent way of showing off its 7cm (3in) long, highly decorative, heart-shaped, silver-spotted leaves. Do not confuse it with *Epipremnum aureum* (*see p. 122*), which is justifiably called the devil's ivy because in its native Solomon Islands it can sprint up to 12m (40ft) high (though it will only reach one-quarter of that indoors). Water freely when in full growth, applying a monthly liquid feed; water moderately in winter. Spray regularly to create some humidity. Susceptible to scale insects and red spider mites.

PLANT PROFILE

HEIGHT 45–90cm (18–36in) or more

SITE Full or bright filtered light

SOIL John Innes No. 3

HARDINESS Min 15°C (59°F)

S

Sedum morganianum Stonecrop

AN EXTRAORDINARY MEXICAN SUCCULENT, this sedum has a
perpetual bad hair day, with a mass of thick trailing stems that
dangle over the side of its pot. To get the full effect, grow it in
a hanging basket (*see inset*), where its pale green leaves, which are
tightly clustered on the long stems, can be clearly seen. With luck,
in summer, there will be small, pink, star-shaped flowers at the tips
of the stems. Keep out of direct summer sun and water moderately
when in full growth, applying a monthly, half-strength liquid feed;
water sparingly in winter. Beware of overwatering, which is fatal.
Look out for aphids, scale insects and mealybugs.

OTHER VARIETY *S. sieboldii* (a much more modest Japanese sedum
that just about trails over the edge of a pot).

PLANT PROFILE
HEIGHT 30cm (12in)
SPREAD 60–90cm (24in–3ft)
SITE Full light
SOIL John Innes No. 2
HARDINESS Min 5-7°C (41–45°F)
FLOWERING Spring and summer

Selaginella kraussiana Krauss's spikemoss

S

A CURIOUS, LITTLE SOUTH AFRICAN PLANT, Krauss's spikemoss hugs the ground with mossy, bright evergreen tufts and grows out in all directions, rooting into the soil as it goes. It can be used to provide very effective ground cover in a conservatory border, or grown in a pot (*see inset*) or terrarium (an enclosed glass or plastic container for plants), but take care to keep its spread under control. It demands high levels of humidity and a place out of direct sun. Water freely using rainwater or soft water when in full growth, and apply a monthly liquid feed; keep just moist in winter.

OTHER VARIETIES *S. kraussiana* 'Aurea' (yellow-green foliage); *S. kraussiana* 'Variegata' (leaves with creamy markings).

PLANT PROFILE
HEIGHT 5cm (2in)
SPREAD 30 60cm (12–24in)
SITE Bright filtered light
SOIL John Innes No. 2
HARDINESS Min 5–7°C (41–45°F)

S | *Senecio articulatus* 'Variegatus' Candle plant

THIS QUIRKY, QUICK-GROWING, spreading African succulent has fleshy, silvery-blue stems made up of jointed, separate segments that poke up out of the ground. The blue-green leaves and flowerheads are a bonus with their bold pink or cream marks, while the creamy-white flowers, which look good and last well, have an appalling smell. 'Variegatus' grows over winter and is dormant in summer. In winter, provide low humidity and water moderately, applying a monthly, half-strength liquid feed; keep just moist when dormant. Good ventilation is important. Beware whiteflies, aphids and red spider mites.

OTHER VARIETY *S. articulatus* (without the bold pink or cream marks).

PLANT PROFILE

HEIGHT 30cm (12in)

SPREAD Over 60cm (24in)

SITE Full light

SOIL 2 parts John Innes No. 1, 1 leafmould and grit

HARDINESS Min 7°C (45°F)

FLOWERING Summer to autumn

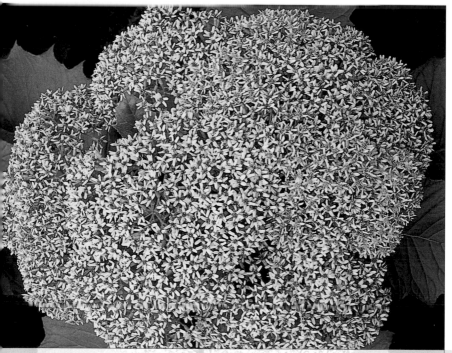

Senecio grandiflorus

S

THE CHUNKY, MEXICAN SHRUB, *S. grandiflorus,* tends to be rather rounded when young but becomes increasingly erect as it matures. The purple stems carry its big attraction – large, splendid leaves, which are up to 25cm (10in) long and rusty-brown on the underside. Poking up, just above these leaves, are the clustered packs of tiny yellow summer flowers. It needs bright light and plenty of space in a conservatory border to thrive. Water moderately when in growth, applying a monthly liquid feed; keep just moist over the winter. Protect against whiteflies, aphids and red spider mites.

PLANT PROFILE

HEIGHT 2m (6ft)

SPREAD 1.2m (4ft)

SITE Full light

SOIL 2 parts John Innes No. 1 to 1 part leafmould and grit

HARDINESS Min 7–10°C (45–50°F)

FLOWERING Winter

S | *Senecio rowleyanus* String of beads

STRING OF BEADS IS GROWN for its long, thin, stringy stems, which tumble over the sides of a hanging basket. They are covered with hundreds of tiny, pea-like leaves, creating a kind of see-through beaded curtain. The small, white flowers usually appear in late summer and develop right at the end of the 90cm (3ft) stems. Good ventilation is important, as is moderate watering when in full growth with a monthly, half-strength liquid feed; keep just moist over the winter months. Prone to whiteflies, aphids and red spider mites.

PLANT PROFILE

HEIGHT To 90cm (3ft)

SPREAD 30cm (12in)

SITE Full light

SOIL 2 parts John Innes No. 1 to 1 part leafmould and grit

HARDINESS Min 7–10°C (45–50°F)

FLOWERING Summer

Selenicereus grandiflorus Queen of the night

S

THIS CLIMBING CACTUS has magnificent, sweetly-scented, white flowers (unfortunately not that prolific), which open up at night. The finger-thin, tube-like stems (*see inset*) have aerial roots which, in the wild, grab hold of a host plant; in conservatories they are best grown against a trellis to provide support. Growth is quite fast – it will reach 2m (8ft) high after five years – but it can be kept in check by pruning in the growing season (but not when dormant in winter). Provide average to high humidity and water freely in summer, applying a monthly, half-strength liquid feed; keep just moist in winter. Beware scale insects and mealybugs.

OTHER VARIETY *S. anthonyanus* (30cm/12in high and wide-spreading, with nocturnal yellowish or creamy-white flowers).

PLANT PROFILE
HEIGHT 5m (15ft)
SITE Bright indirect light
SOIL Epiphytic cactus compost
HARDINESS Min 15°C (59°F)
FLOWERING Summer

S | *Sinningia speciosa* 'Red Flicker' Florists' gloxinia

SINNINGIAS HAVE FLOWERS that range in colour from white to rich purple. 'Red Flicker' has a characteristic array of soft, fleshy, green leaves that tend to point out sideways, and trumpet-shaped flowers up to 5cm (2in) long that appear intermittently all summer. Plants need careful treatment – water moderately when in full growth, applying a half-strength liquid tomato feed every two weeks. As the leaves turn yellow and die in the autumn, gradually cease watering; keep the compost dry over winter and place the pot in a cool, dry place. Start into growth next spring (if repotting, keep the tuber hollow side up), with moderate watering, in a warmer room.

OTHER VARIETIES *S.* 'Hollywood' (blue flowers); *S.* 'Emperor Frederich' (red, edged-white flowers); *S.* 'Violacea' (violet flowers).

PLANT PROFILE	
HEIGHT 30cm (12in)	
SPREAD 30cm (12in)	
SITE Bright filtered light	
SOIL Loamless compost	
HARDINESS Min 15ºC (59°F)	
FLOWERING Summer	

Smithiantha 'Orange King' Temple Bells

S

AN EXTREMELY USEFUL POT PLANT, 'Orange King' has green, heart-shaped leaves covered in reddish hairs, with dark red veins. Its profusion of small, summer flowers, which resemble dangling bells, are red on the outside, with red-spotted, orange throats. High humidity is important, as is moderate (not excessive) watering when in full growth, with a quarter-strength liquid tomato feed with each drink. Also provide a constant temperature of 19°C (66°F). Cease watering over winter, when it needs to be bone dry. The following spring, move it into a slightly larger pot, add new soil and water sparingly until growth takes off. Susceptible to aphids.

OTHER VARIETY *S. zebrina* (slightly taller with deep green leaves and purple-brown along the veins; scarlet and yellow flowers).

PLANT PROFILE
HEIGHT 60cm (24in)
SPREAD 60cm (24in)
SITE Bright filtered light
SOIL Loamless compost
HARDINESS Min 10°C (50°F)
FLOWERING Summer to autumn

S | *Solanum pseudocapsicum* Christmas cherry

WIDELY SOLD IN THE RUN-UP to Christmas, this bushy, evergreen pot plant has star-shaped, white summer flowers followed by an excellent covering of oval, long-lasting, red, yellow or orange-red fruit. It is easily grown, and should be watered freely in full growth, with a monthly liquid feed. Place it outside over summer in a sheltered, lightly-shaded position and mist over the flowers to help the fruit set. Bring it indoors for the autumn, and water sparingly when dormant over winter. Cut back the stems by half when the show of berries declines, and repot next spring. Beware aphids and red spider mites. Emphasize to children that the fruit is toxic.

OTHER VARIETY *S. capsicastrum* (the winter cherry has bright red or orange-red fruit).

PLANT PROFILE

HEIGHT 30–45cm (12–18in)

SPREAD 30–45cm (12–18in)

SITE Full light

SOIL John Innes No. 2

HARDINESS Min 7–10°C (45–50°F)

FLOWERING Summer

Solanum wendlandii Potato vine

S

AN EXCEPTIONAL, SCRAMBLING CLIMBER with a big show of colour, the potato vine needs space when grown in a conservatory border, but can easily be restricted to 2m (6ft) high in a pot. The showy bunches of small lilac-blue flowers, with wide-open petals, last for many weeks. Tie in the growth to horizontal wall wires, and provide shade from hot sun and average humidity. Water freely when in full growth, applying a monthly liquid feed; water sparingly when dormant. Wear gloves when cutting back the sideshoots in early spring (leaving three to four buds) because of its nasty hooks, used for support. Beware aphids and red spider mites. All parts are toxic.

OTHER VARIETY *S. jasminoides* (a half-hardy vine that is slightly taller with blue-white scented flowers).

PLANT PROFILE
HEIGHT 5m (15ft) or more
SPREAD 2m (6ft)
SITE Full light
SOIL John Innes No. 2
HARDINESS Min 7–10°C (45–50°F)
FLOWERING Summer

S | *Soleirolia soleirolii* Baby's tears, Mind-your-own-business

AN INVETERATE, NON-STOP INVADER that is extremely easy to grow, baby's tears keeps on coming – it can cover a wide area outside (where it is perfectly hardy) and a conservatory border inside, creating a green mat beneath taller, more striking plants. Because it likes free-draining soil, mix in horticultural grit to help open it up. When it is in full growth over summer, baby's tears should be watered liberally, but in winter, water it much more sparingly. If it is being grown in a pot (where it produces an attractive green mound), water it from below.

OTHER VARIETIES *S. soleirolii* 'Aurea' (gold-green leaves); *S. soleirolii* 'Variegata' (silver markings on the leaves).

PLANT PROFILE

HEIGHT 5cm (2in)

SPREAD 30cm (12in)

SITE Bright light

SOIL John Innes No. 1

HARDINESS Fully hardy

FLOWERING Summer

Solenostemon 'Crimson Ruffles' Coleus

 S

COLEUS MAKE SUPERB FOLIAGE PLANTS and can be grown in pots or borders to add a lively, jazzy note. The leaves range from black to yellow with red speckles – 'Crimson Ruffles' has blood-red leaves and purple veins. The mixed annual coleus plants are thrown out in the autumn but the larger, named kind (eg, 'Pineapple Beauty') are kept. Nip out the shoots in the spring for extra leafy growth and, because the flowers are insignificant, snip off the buds. Water freely in full growth and add a high-nitrogen liquid feed (promoting even more leaves) every two weeks; keep just moist in winter. Repot in the spring. Beware mealybugs, scale insects and whiteflies.

OTHER VARIETIES *S.* 'Pineapple Beauty' (yellow-green leaves turn gold); *S.* 'Royal Scot' (yellow-edged, red leaves, green-brown centres).

PLANT PROFILE
HEIGHT 60cm (24in)
SPREAD 60cm (24in)
SITE Bright filtered light
SOIL John Innes No. 3
HARDINESS Min 4°C (39°F)
FLOWERING Any time

S | *Sollya heterophylla* Bluebell creeper

A MODEST, AUSTRALIAN, EVERGREEN CLIMBER, bluebell creeper can be grown in a pot or conservatory border. It invariably looks best when allowed to creep through adjacent plants that act as a support (alternatively, train it up canes or a set of wires). The thin stems carry narrow leaves and dangling clusters of bell-shaped, blue flowers that give a long display when given constant warmth – they are followed by small, round, blue berries. Provide shade from hot sun, and water moderately over summer, adding a monthly liquid feed; water sparingly in winter. Red spider mites may be a problem.

PLANT PROFILE

HEIGHT 2m (6ft)

SPREAD 1.2m (4ft)

SITE Full light

SOIL John Innes No. 2

HARDINESS Half hardy (borderline)

FLOWERING Early summer to autumn

Sparrmannia africana African hemp

S

THIS VIGOROUS, EVERGREEN, SOUTH AFRICAN SHRUB has large, virtually triangular, hairy leaves that are fresh green (*see inset*) – they combine well with the cup-shaped, white flowers, which have bright yellow stamens. It can easily grow up to 6m (20ft) if allowed, but an annual prune after flowering will keep it at a much more manageable size. Either way, it needs plenty of space in a conservatory border. Water freely when in full growth and apply a monthly liquid feed; water much more sparingly in winter. Beware whiteflies and red spider mites.

OTHER VARIETY   *S. africana* 'Variegata' (leaves with white markings).

PLANT PROFILE
HEIGHT 2m (6ft)
SPREAD 1.2m (4ft)
SITE Full light
SOIL John Innes No. 3
HARDINESS Min 7°C (45°F)
FLOWERING Late spring and early summer

S

Spathiphyllum 'Mauna Loa' Peace lily

AN EXTRAORDINARY PLANT, whose relatives grow in tropical forests in the Americas and Indonesia, the peace lily has beautiful, glossy, dark green leaves up to 30cm (12in) long (*see inset*), and superb flowers. With 'Mauna Loa', what looks like a large, semi-circular, white petal is a spathe (a conspicuous, hood-like bract) – the central spike (the spadix) has the tiny, white flowers growing all around it. The peace lily may be grown as an eye-catcher in a pot, or in the conservatory border as a gap filler. It needs high humidity, warmth and some shade or the sun will burn the foliage. Water well over summer, adding a monthly liquid feed; water sparingly over winter.

OTHER VARIETIES *S.* 'Sensation' (larger, more exotic leaves); *S. wallisii* (slightly smaller flowers).

PLANT PROFILE
HEIGHT 1m (3ft)
SPREAD 60cm (24in)
SITE Bright indirect light
SOIL John Innes No. 2
HARDINESS Min 15°C (59°F)
FLOWERING Spring and summer

Stephanotis floribunda variegata Madagascar jasmine

S

ONE OF THE MOST INCREDIBLY-SCENTED CLIMBERS, Madagascar jasmine has gorgeous, thick, white, star-shaped flowers about 2.5cm (1in) long on stiff, woody stems. They can be trained up a wall (against horizontal wires) or around a pillar. The leathery, dark green variegated leaves are an added attraction, and grow up to 10cm (4in) long. It is tricky to grow and must be kept at about 18°C (65°F), with decent humidity in a draught-free place; also provide some shade from direct, scorching sun. Water freely when in full growth, applying a liquid feed every two to three weeks; water sparingly in winter. Beware red spider mites, scale insects and mealybugs.

OTHER VARIETY *S. floribunda* (plain, dark green leaves).

PLANT PROFILE
HEIGHT 1–4m (3–12ft)
SITE Full light
SOIL John Innes No. 3
HARDINESS Min 15°C (59°F)
FLOWERING Spring to autumn

S | *Strelitzia reginae* Crane flower, Bird of Paradise

THE TEMPTATION TO BUY the crane flower is enormous because from side-on, its flowers resemble a fabulous green and red-beaked bird with an orange-crested top. Be warned, however, that small plants become very big clumps and take up plenty of room. Plants also need to be about six years old before they start flowering. Stand in bright light, but shade it from direct, scorching sun, and ventilate well when temperatures exceed 20°C (68°F). Water freely over summer and apply a monthly liquid feed; water sparingly over winter. Repot every second year. Susceptible to scale insects.

OTHER VARIETY *S. reginae* 'Humilis' (the best choice if there is limited space – it grows 80cm/32in high and is happy in a pot).

PLANT PROFILE
HEIGHT To 2m (6ft)
SPREAD 1m (3ft)
SITE Full light
SOIL John Innes No. 3
HARDINESS Min 10°C (50°F)
FLOWERING Winter to spring

Streptocarpus 'Lisa' Cape primrose

S

A TYPICAL CAPE PRIMROSE, 'Lisa' has clusters of shell pink flowers with white throats. It blooms over a long period, giving extremely good value for money – promptly remove the fading flowers to encourage more buds to form. The wrinkled, strap-shaped leaves, which form a rosette, have a fine covering of hairs. Water freely when in growth and apply a liquid tomato feed every two weeks, but note that it is vital to allow the compost to dry out before the plant has its next drink; keep just moist in winter. Repot every spring. Prone to mealybugs.

OTHER VARIETIES *S.* 'Cynthia' (red flowers); *S.* 'Heidi' (blue flowers with purple markings); *S.* 'Nicola' (deep pink flowers); *S.* 'Sarah' (dark purple flowers).

PLANT PROFILE
HEIGHT 20cm (8in)
SPREAD 35cm (14in)
SITE Bright filtered light
SOIL Loamless compost
HARDINESS Min 10°C (50°F)
FLOWERING Spring to autumn

S | *Streptosolen jamesonii* Marmalade bush

THIS DASHING, SOUTH AMERICAN EVERGREEN SHRUB is a mix
of solid, chunky growth and dangling, trailing, outer stems, with
a bright show of yellow to orange-yellow flowers. The best place
for it is in a conservatory border, trained against a wall where it will
exceed 2.4m (8ft); with annual pruning after flowering, it can be
kept at this height (or less in a pot). When pruning, cut back
flowered shoots to within two to four buds of the permanent
framework. Provide shade from direct, scorching sun, water freely
when in growth and add a monthly liquid feed; water sparingly in
winter. Protect against aphids, whiteflies and red spider mites.

OTHER VARIETY *S. jamesonii* 'Fire Gold' (golden-yellow flowers
flowers and fresh green leaves).

PLANT PROFILE
HEIGHT 2.4m (8ft)
SPREAD 1.2m (4ft)
SITE Full light
SOIL John Innes No. 3
HARDINESS Min 7°C (45°F)
FLOWERING Late spring to late summer

Strobilanthes dyeriana Persian shield

AN ORNAMENTAL, EVERGREEN FOLIAGE PLANT, Persian shield is often grown for its pairs of stiff, outward-pointing, lance-shaped leaves that are silvery-purple with prominent, dark green veins. When it loses its compact, bushy shape after about 18 months and becomes straggly, replace it with a cutting taken in the spring or summer. When this young plant starts growing well, occasionally nip off the growing tips to force out more stems and extra leaves. The pale blue, autumn flowers are a plus. Keep it out of direct, scorching sun, and water freely when in full growth, adding a monthly liquid feed; water moderately over winter. Beware red spider mites.

OTHER VARIETY *S. atropurpureus* (dark green, nettle-like leaves with an airy scattering of purple or indigo flowers; 1.5m/5ft high, hardy).

PLANT PROFILE	
HEIGHT	1.2m (4ft)
SPREAD	1m (3ft)
SITE	Full light
SOIL	John Innes No. 2
HARDINESS	Min 12°C (54°F)
FLOWERING	Autumn

S

Syngonium podophyllum Goosefoot

GOOSEFOOT IS ALSO CALLED the arrowhead plant because the leaves change shape and, in the second stage, are roughly triangular before they start dividing into sections. At various times, different shapes are simultaneously evident on the same plant. The stems like to grab hold of a support (in the wild, a tree) to climb up, but they are happy with mossy poles in a pot or border (*see inset*). Ideally give the plant hot, humid conditions; although it will survive without them, some humidity is important. Water freely when in full growth, applying a liquid feed every three to four weeks; water moderately in winter. Beware mealybugs and red spider mites.

OTHER VARIETIES *S. podophyllum* 'Trileaf Wonder' (silver-grey, veined leaves); *S. podophyllum* 'Variegatum' (creamy-white markings).

PLANT PROFILE
HEIGHT 1–1.2m (3–4ft)
SITE Bright indirect light
SOIL Loamless compost
HARDINESS Min 15°C (59°F)
FLOWERING Summer

Tetrastigma voinierianum Chestnut vine

THIS POTENTIAL GIANT of an evergreen climber can hit 15m (50ft) in the wild in Laos, and will reach half that in a conservatory where you must prune it hard to keep it in check. When allowed to romp up the horizontal wires on a wall, which it clings on to with its tendrils, this vine creates a sheet of virtually diamond-shaped, green leaves. Further restrict its growth by keeping it in a pot, and by providing less than ideal conditions (ie, not hot and humid). Note that the Chestnut vine must be watered freely in summer, with a monthly liquid feed; water moderately over winter.

PLANT PROFILE

HEIGHT 2m (6ft) upwards

SITE Bright filtered light

SOIL John Innes No. 3

HARDINESS Min 15°C (59°F)

FLOWERING Summer

T | *Thunbergia alata* Black-eyed Susan

IT IS WELL WORTH GROWING the annual black-eyed Susan in the border to let the climbing stems charge over adjoining shrubs, run up canes and wires, and twine through other climbers. The wide-faced, bright orange or yellow flowers have five petals with a black dot in the centre. Nothing special, nothing exotic, but it is cheery and good fun (*see inset*). Sow seed at 16–18°C (61–64°F) in the spring and, when the young plants are ready, plant them in the border. Water freely over summer, applying a monthly liquid feed. Rip out the plants after flowering and discard. Protect against red spider mites and scale insects.

OTHER VARIETY *T. gregorii* (from tropical Africa, may be grown as an annual or perennial; reaches 3m/10ft high with clear orange flowers).

PLANT PROFILE

HEIGHT To 2.5m (8ft)

SITE Full light

SOIL John Innes No. 3

HARDINESS Min 7–10°C (45–50°F)

FLOWERING Summer to autumn

Thunbergia grandiflora Blue trumpet vine

T

THIS MAGNIFICENT, VIGOROUS, north Indian, woody-stemmed, twining climber can easily reach up to 6m (20ft). It has two big attractions: dark green, heart-shaped evergreen leaves that are about 10cm (4in) long and softly hairy; and pale-throated flowers that are an exquisite lavender to violet-blue. The warmer the conditions, the longer it will flower beyond autumn. For a big display, give it a free root run in a border, and provide a sturdy support for it to charge up. If pruning is required, do so in the spring. Water freely over summer, applying a monthly liquid feed; water moderately in winter. Beware red spider mites and scale insects.

OTHER VARIETY *T. mysorensis* (woody-stemmed perennial, 3m/10ft high, with extraordinary, hooded, two-lipped yellow flowers).

PLANT PROFILE

HEIGHT 5m (15ft) or more

SITE Full light

SOIL John Innes No. 3

HARDINESS Min 7–10°C (45–50°F)

FLOWERING Summer to autumn

T | *Tibouchina urvilleana* Brazilian spider flower

THE LARGE, UNMISTAKABLE, 9cm (3½in) wide flowers of the
Brazilian spider flower (also known as glory bush) are the richest
royal purple, and the velvet-like, pointy leaves are equally superb.
The stems are thin and straggly. In a large conservatory, tie them
to horizontal wall wires, but, with more limited space, cut back
the stems in mid-spring, leaving two buds on each to create a
more compact shape. Water freely during full growth, giving
a monthly liquid feed; water sparingly in winter. Protect against
red spider mites and aphids. It is often listed in books and sold as
T. semidecandra.

OTHER VARIETIES *T. urvilleana* 'Edwardsii' (large, purple flowers on
a compact bush); *T. urvilleana* 'Jules' (60cm/24in high with blue flowers).

PLANT PROFILE

HEIGHT To 2.5m (8ft)

SPREAD To 1.5m (5ft)

SITE Full light

SOIL John Innes No. 3

HARDINESS Min 3–5°C
(39–41°F)

FLOWERING Summer to
autumn

Tillandsia multicaulis Air plant

IN THE WILD, this Central American air plant is found attached to the bark of trees, where it produces beautiful, blue flowers from red segments. It absorbs moisture in the air and the roots function like an anchor. It is often sold with its roots and base wrapped in sphagnum moss and encircled by wire, which is attached to a length of bark – in a conservatory, hang it up on a wall or dangle it from the ceiling. Provide moderate to high humidity by spraying around it at least twice a day with rain- or soft water. If the conservatory gets cold and damp in winter, cease spraying or the plant might rot and die.

OTHER VARIETY *T. fasciculata* (white and purple flowers emerging from red to yellow segments).

T

PLANT PROFILE

HEIGHT 40cm (16in)

SPREAD 40cm (16in)

SITE Bright indirect light

SOIL Sphagnum moss

HARDINESS Min 7°C (45°F)

FLOWERING Late spring

T *Tillandsia stricta* Air plant

FROM VENEZUELA DOWN TO NORTHERN ARGENTINA, this air plant forms clumps on the bark of trees, producing pale green leaves and, in spring, spikes with about 40 blue or purple flowers. It does not like being grown in pots and prefers to have its roots and base wrapped up in sphagnum moss, which is then encircled by wire and attached to a length of bark. In a conservatory, hang it up on a wall or dangle it from the ceiling. Provide moderate to high humidity by spraying around it twice a day (or more), with rain- or soft water. If the conservatory gets cold and damp in winter, cease spraying – when the plant becomes too wet, it may rot.

OTHER VARIETY *T. argentea* (rosettes of silvery, pale green leaves and bright red or blue flowers).

PLANT PROFILE
HEIGHT 10–20cm (4–8in)
SPREAD 10–20cm (4–8in))
SITE Bright indirect light
SOIL Sphagnum moss
HARDINESS Min 7°C (45°F)
FLOWERING Spring

Tolmiea menziesii Thousand mothers

T

THE APTLY-NAMED THOUSAND MOTHERS (also known as the piggyback plant) produces young plants right at the base of the older leaves, gradually weighing them down (*see inset*). Snip off these plantlets from mid- to late summer, and plant them in multi-purpose compost, where they will quickly take root. They will then produce a mound of kidney-shaped, pale to lime-green, hairy leaves with conspicuous veins and, in late spring, barely-scented, greenish-purple flowers that are its least attractive feature. Water freely when in full growth and apply a monthly liquid feed; water sparingly in winter.

OTHER VARIETY *T. menziesii* 'Taff's Gold' (paler green leaves with cream and pale yellow markings; keep out of scorching sun).

PLANT PROFILE

HEIGHT 30cm (12in)

SPREAD 1m (3ft)

SITE Bright filtered light

SOIL John Innes No. 2

HARDINESS Fully hardy

FLOWERING Late spring and early summer

T

Trachycarpus wagnerianus

A MUCH SMALLER VERSION of the Chusan palm (*T. fortunei*), which is famed for its splayed-open, fan-like leaves, *T. wagnerianus* is slightly different because it has much more elegant, rigid leaves that do not flop. Like the Chusan palm, it has clusters of yellow flowers in early summer and is hardy enough to be grown outside in mild, sheltered regions of north-west Europe. In a conservatory it will grow quite tall (which takes time because it is slow growing, especially if placed in a pot) and eventually it will need to be moved outside. Although rarely mentioned in gardening books, it is readily available from specialist nurseries. Water well over the summer months, and more sparingly in winter.

PLANT PROFILE

HEIGHT 3m (10ft)

SPREAD 1.2m (4ft)

SITE Bright light

SOIL John Innes No. 2

HARDINESS Frost hardy

FLOWERING Early summer

Tradescantia spathacea Three-men-in-a-boat

THIS NON-TRAILING TRADESCANTIA makes highly-effective clumps of rosettes with its angled up, fleshy, pointy leaves (*see inset*) that are dark green above and deep purple beneath. The white flowers pop out of purple segments that hang on for months at a time. Although it can be grown in a pot, it is much more effective when given the freedom to spread across a conservatory border to create a low background for taller, high-performance, dominant plants. Water moderately while in full growth, applying a monthly liquid feed; water sparingly over winter.

OTHER VARIETY *T. spathacea* 'Vittata' (leaves with several pale yellow stripes).

PLANT PROFILE
HEIGHT 30cm (12in)
SPREAD 30cm (12in)
SITE Bright filtered light
SOIL John Innes No. 2
HARDINESS Min 10–16°C (50–61°F)
FLOWERING Summer

T

T

Tradescantia zebrina 'Purpusii' Wandering Jew

ONE OF THE MOST POPULAR tradescantias for its extremely attractive mix of colours, 'Purpusii' makes a good pot or hanging basket plant although it can also be used very effectively in a conservatory border to cover the soil beneath taller, feature plants. The stems are greenish, the leaves rich bronze-purple, and the flowers pink. Extremely easy to grow, it helps if the stems are nipped out in the spring to encourage more colourful growth. It should be watered moderately while in full growth, with a monthly liquid feed; water sparingly over winter.

OTHER VARIETY *T. zebrina* (leaves with a green, central stripe flanked by silver stripes, and purple underneath); *T. zebrina* 'Quadricolor' (leaves striped green, cream, pink and silver – *see inset*).

PLANT PROFILE
HEIGHT 15cm (6in)
SPREAD 20cm (8in)
SITE Bright filtered light
SOIL John Innes No. 2
HARDINESS Min 10–16°C (50–61°F)
FLOWERING Summer

Tripogandra multiflora

A CREEPING-TRAILING PERENNIAL with a light scattering of infrequent, small, three petalled white, or sometimes pink, flowers, *T. multiflora* is chiefly grown for its dainty, airy look. Grow it in a small, coloured pot and let the growth dangle over the sides. It is easy to look after, but needs shelter from the midday summer sun, with regular summer watering and an occasional all-purpose feed; Provide a moderate supply of water in winter when it needs to be kept on the dry side. This perennial originates in western tropical South America to Costa Rica, and appreciates an occasional misting to create some humidity.

PLANT PROFILE
HEIGHT 30–45cm (12–18in)
SPREAD 30–45cm (12–18in)
SITE Full light
SOIL John Innes No. 2
HARDINESS Min 12°C (54°F)
FLOWERING Intermittently

T

T

Tweedia caerulea

THIS WEAKLY TWINING, EVERGREEN, shrubby, South American climber has almost fleshy, star-shaped, sky-blue flowers that end up purple. They emerge from buds that have a pink flush, while the hairy, light green leaves are heart-shaped. It can be grown in a pot to be placed outside over summer, or to stand against a conservatory wall where the stems can be tied to horizontal wires so that the flowers are more clearly seen. Prune it in spring, leaving two to four buds on the branches of the main framework to encourage plenty of new vigorous shoots. Water freely over summer, giving a monthly liquid feed; water sparingly in winter.

PLANT PROFILE

HEIGHT 60–90cm (24–36in)

SITE Full light

SOIL John Innes No. 2

HARDINESS Min 3–5°C (39–41°F)

FLOWERING Summer to early autumn

Veltheimia bracteata

A STRIKING, SOUTH AFRICAN BULB, *V. bracteata* has a marvellous rosette of thick, strappy, shiny leaves that grow up to 35cm (14in) long. Its distinctive, spring flowers grow in clusters of up to about 60 narrow, pinkish-purple tubes, right at the tip of its purple-green stems. Plant the bulbs in late summer to early autumn, leaving the tips poking above the soil (add horticultural grit to make it more free-draining). Keep in a cool place and water sparingly. When growth appears, increase watering, adding a liquid feed every two weeks. Once the leaves fade, reduce watering, keeping just moist when dormant. Repot when the container is packed with roots.

OTHER VARIETY *V. bracteata* 'Rosalba' (yellowish flowers with a red tinge; no dormant period).

PLANT PROFILE
HEIGHT 45cm (18in)
SPREAD 30cm (12in)
SITE Full sun
SOIL John Innes No. 2
HARDINESS Min 5–7°C (41–45°F)
FLOWERING Late winter and early spring

V | *Vitis vinifera* 'Muscat Hamburgh' Grape vine

THERE IS A TERRIFIC RANGE of black and white greenhouse grapes, but they need hot, dry summers to crop well. Train them up the walls and along the roof of a conservatory, planting them against horizontal wires set 22–30cm (9–12in) away from the glass. Cut back the stem by two-thirds on planting, and thereafter train growth upwards and outwards, giving an annual prune; the eventual height and spread depends on the training and pruning regime. If space is limited, buy 1.2m (4ft) standard pot plants. Ventilate well in winter, creating cold conditions, but from late winter provide a warmer environment, and fresh air to combat mildew. Water in dry periods.

OTHER VARIETIES *V. vinifera* 'Muscat of Hungary' (thick bunches of mid-season white grapes with a good flavour).

PLANT PROFILE
HEIGHT To 7.5m (25ft)
SPREAD To 7.5m (25ft)
SITE Full sun
SOIL Reasonably fertile and free-draining
HARDINESS Fully hardy
FLOWERING Summer

Vriesia hieroglyphica King of the Bromeliads

V

THIS SUPERB, BRAZILIAN PLANT has a rosette of outward-pointing, yellowish-green leaves with attractive, dark green patterning that looks a bit like ancient hieroglyphics. In summer, it has extraordinary, erect, greenish-yellow growths (called bracts), about 75cm (30in) high, with small, sulphur-yellow flowers. The easiest way to grow it is in a pot of special compost. When in full growth (through spring and summer), keep the central rosette filled with rain- or soft water, applying a quarter-strength nitrogen feed every four to five weeks; keep just moist in winter. Beware scale insects.

OTHER VARIETY *V. splendens* (the flaming sword has red bracts and yellow flowers; leaves have dark green, purple or reddish-brown bands).

PLANT PROFILE
HEIGHT To 1m (3ft)
SPREAD To 1m (3ft)
SITE Moderate light
SOIL Epiphytic bromeliad compost
HARDINESS Min 15°C (59°F)
FLOWERING Summer

V x *Vuylstekeara* Cambria 'Plush'

AN UNPRONOUNCEABLE NAME (something like Vwheel-stek-ee-ara) for an easily-grown, flamboyant, crimson orchid with a red-speckled, large, white lip. It flowers possibly twice a year, on a 40–50cm (16–20in) long spike, once in late spring and again in the autumn (*see inset*). Avoid direct, scorching sun and draughts, and create good humidity. Never let 'Plush' dry out completely (but do not let it become waterlogged), and add a light, liquid orchid feed over the summer. Do not be tempted to rush it into a large pot – keep it in the smallest one that will accommodate its roots.

OTHER VARIETY x *V*. Cambria 'Lensing's Favourite' (with yellow flowers).

PLANT PROFILE

HEIGHT 30cm (12in)

SPREAD 8cm (3in)

SITE Bright light

SOIL Standard orchid compost

HARDINESS Min 10–13°C (50–55°F)

FLOWERING Late spring and autumn

Washingtonia robusta Thread palm

A GIANT IN THE WILDS OF MEXICO, where it can reach 25m (80ft), the thread palm will shoot up quite high in a conservatory and require plenty of space. It will grow more slowly in a pot, but eventually it is a case of putting it outside in summer (where it will die the following winter), and starting again inside with a little one. Its incredible trunk consists of what look like large, overlapping scales, and spurting out of the top are long, sharply-toothed stalks with huge, fan-shaped leaves at the ends. Add leafmould and sharp sand to the soil in the pot, and water moderately over summer, giving a monthly liquid feed; keep almost dry in winter.

OTHER VARIETY *W. filifera* (another potential giant, with toothed leaf stalks and greyish-green, fan-shaped leaves).

PLANT PROFILE
HEIGHT 3m (10ft) or more
SPREAD 2m (6ft)
SITE Full light
SOIL John Innes No. 3
HARDINESS Min 8–10°C (46–50°F)
FLOWERING Summer

Y | *Yucca elephantipes* Giant yucca

THE YUCCAS ARE SERIOUS PLANTS with fantastic presence and enormous, strapping, stiff leaves, many with needle-vicious tips at the end. The long-leaved giant yucca is not dangerous (being spineless), and tends to resemble a swollen-stemmed shrub or miniature tree, with a few branches emerging from lower down. To get a mature plant to flower, place it outside over summer, but bring it back in again at the start of autumn. Water moderately when in full growth, applying a monthly liquid feed; water sparingly in winter. If it is being planted outdoors over summer, a hot spot with free-draining soil is important.

OTHER VARIETY *Y. aloifolia* (the Spanish bayonet has lethal needles at the ends of the leaves – not for children).

PLANT PROFILE

HEIGHT 2m (6ft)

SPREAD 2m (6ft)

SITE Full light

SOIL John Innes No. 2

HARDINESS Min 10°C (50°F)

FLOWERING Mid- and late summer

Zantedeschia elliottiana Golden arum

WITH ITS MAGNIFICENT, almost triangular, dark green, spotted leaves that stand smartly upright, and its beautiful, yellow flowers (called spadices), golden arum makes a superb conservatory plant (*see inset*). It is remarkably easy to grow and should be watered freely when in full growth, with an added liquid feed every two weeks until the flowers have faded (remove the leaves at this point). Keep just moist over winter when it is dormant. Repot in the spring, keeping the underground portion just under the soil surface, and gradually increase the watering while initially raising the temperature closer to 16°C (60°F) before the conservatory heats up in the summer.

OTHER VARIETY *Z. aethiopica* (the frost-hardy arum lily has bright green leaves and large, pure white flowers known as spathes).

PLANT PROFILE

HEIGHT 60–90cm (24–36in)

SPREAD 20cm (8in)

SITE Full light

SOIL John Innes No. 2

HARDINESS Min 10°C (50°F)

FLOWERING Summer

The publisher would like to thank the following for their kind permission to reproduce their photographs:

(Abbreviations key; t=top, b=below, r=right, l=left, c=centre, a=above, DK=DK Images)

16: DK /Roger Smith; **18:** DK/Roger Smith; **31:** Garden World Images; **37:** Photos Horticultural; 39: DK/Roger Smith (c); **55:** Garden World Images; **59:** DK/Roger Smith; **65:** Garden Picture Library/Philippe Bonduel; **71:** Garden Picture Library (tl); **82:** Garden Picture Library/Howard Rice; **83:** Garden Picture Library/Howard Rice (tr), John Glover (tc); **86:** DK/Roger Smith; **98:** DK/Roger Smith; **99:** DK/Roger Smith; **105:** DK/Roger Smith; **107:** A-Z Botanical Collection/Jennifer Fry; **110:** Photos Horticultural; **113:** A-Z Botanical Collection/F Merket (c); **114:** Garden Picture Library/Mel Watson; **116:** A-Z Botanical Collection/Andrew Cowin; **121:** Photos Horticultural; **122:** A-Z Botanical Collection/Mrs W Monks; **148:** A-Z Botanical Collection (c), Garden World Images (tl); **151:** Garden Picture Library/Howard Rice; **154:** DK/Roger Smith; **157:** A-Z Botanical Collection/Geoff Kidd; **160:** DK/Andrew Butler; **162:** Garden World Images; **163:** DK/Roger Smith; **164:** A-Z Botanical Collection/Neil Davis; **167:** A-Z Botanical Collection/A Young; 170: Garden Picture Library/Christopher Fairweather; **172:** Jerry Harpur; **173:** Jerry Harpur; **174:** DK/Roger Smith (c);

175: A-Z Botanical Collection/K Jayaram (c); **176:** Garden Picture Library/Friedrich Strauss; **177:** DK/Roger Smith; **186:** Garden Picture Library/John Glover; **187:** A-Z Botanical Collection (c); **189:** Garden Picture Library/Friedrich Strauss; **190:** Garden Matters/Steffie Shields; **191:** A-Z Botanical Collection/Geoff Kidd; **192:** Photos Horticultural; **193:** DK/Roger Smith (c); **194:** Garden Matters/J Feltwell; **195:** Andrew Lawson; **196:** DK/Roger Smith; **200:** A-Z Botanical Collection/S Taylor; **203:** Photos Horticultural; **214:** A-Z Botanical Collection/Adrian Thomas; **218:** Jerry Harpur/Plantsman Nursery; **219:** DK/Roger Smith; **223:** DK/Roger Smith; **226:** DK/Roger Smith; **232:** DK/Roger Smith; **252:** Photos Horticultural; **267:** Photos Horticultural; **269:** Garden Matters /J Feltwell; **271:** A-Z Botanical Collection/Mike Danson; **279:** DK/Roger Smith; **284:** Garden Picture Library/Lynne Brotchie; **287:** DK/Roger Smith; **289:** DK/Roger Smith; **290:** DK/Roger Smith; **291:** DK/Roger Smith; **292:** DK/Roger Smith.

All other images © DK Images.

For further information see:
www.dkimages.com